Seat Open

A Memoir of Poker, Degeneracy, and Friendship

Written by Blockhead
Edited by Carrieann Cahall

Copyright © 2018 Blockhead
All rights reserved

Facts have been changed to obscure those involved.

For Mike Neel, who picked up early and left me in the big blind

Table of Contents

Gamble, Gamble 1
Seat Open 16
Chicago Bulls 35
Buffalo Nick and the Champagne Room 46
Ineffective Assistance of Counsel 65
Inheritance 80
ICON 89
The Ruby Dragon Baccarat Championship (2016) 105
The Ruby Dragon Baccarat Championship (2018) 117
Acknowledgements 135
Author Bio 136

Seat Open

Gamble, Gamble

I was eighteen years old living in Las Vegas meaning I knew God as a sucker's bet. Las Vegas was a coal mining town. The unfathomable depths of the Strip held dense, black veins of ore every local saw excavated, hauled off, or burned up for fuel. Luck was the only thing native.

My best friends from high school and I—like everyone else we knew— happily went through life seeing how our fortunes held up throughout the day and expected a refill in the next. We were blissfully unaware of the Las Vegas hierarchy that correctly predicted bad kids grew up running valet, and good kids grew up running the gaming pit. The great kids ran away.

We transitioned from candy-selling and three-card monte games to running a "sports betting service" our senior year of high school. The four of us rushed home at 1:30 every day to drink beer and watch ESPN for a few hours or until we were bored. We looked up the point spreads for NFL games that week and put in bets through one of our listed guardians, usually with a bribe of alcohol. We were convinced we knew what we were doing. Betting based on astrology signs of head coaches would've been more professional.

Despite our "system," our luck ran as hot as the sun, and we made almost a thousand dollars which made us feel like the real-life versions of Ocean's 11. Having just graduated high school, now armed with either a Stations Casino job or local college, it made perfect sense to use all of our gambling winnings to throw an end-of-year hotel party.

We pooled our funds and used a credit card for the deposit. The cardholder was an "adult" who we relied on in a pinch. We booked the SkyLofts at the MGM Grand and

Blockhead

made sure to invite ~70 graduating seniors who liked to party and another ~50 of our friends who hadn't made it to graduation, victims of Las Vegas public education.

On the afternoon of the party, we checked in with luggage filled with Patrón, Grey Goose, mid-shelf weed, mushrooms, three flavors of Doritos, cases of beer, and a bottle of cheap champagne for our friend group. The short-sighted necessities of a high school party. The security guard at the private SkyLoft elevators gave us a funny look, but there was nothing he could do when we presented him with the golden ticket—our room key.

The elevators opened on the 30th floor to a long hallway with a private concierge at the end. Her outfit, skin, and hair were all perfect. A hospitality careerist from Norway or Denmark. We were beyond the reaches of Vegas locals here. She greeted us and handed us off to a personal butler named Mo who assured us anything we would need for the duration of our stay would be taken care of by him, personally. He escorted us into our room.

The name SkyLofts had been disingenuous—this was Heaven.

It was the first two-story hotel room I'd ever been in. Twenty-foot windows captured the entirety of Las Vegas Blvd far below. A carpeted staircase connected an upstairs master bedroom, indoor balcony, and walk-in closet with the infinity tub in an open downstairs bathroom. There was a nine-person dining table with complimentary dragon fruit waiting for us when we walked in. It looked too nice to eat.

Everything about the room was beautiful and appeared brand new. The couch, rugs, and bed all felt like how you wanted them to feel. Once the butler left, we ran all the faucets, ate the fruit, and took an ungodly amount of pictures. It could've been the setting to a rap video, a representation of the pinnacle of success. The four of us— Las Vegas street kids— didn't have the first clue how to treat something so nice.

Seat Open

In small groups, or one-by-one, our guests arrived. One of our four would receive a call and head down to the lobby to escort our guests in past security. As we repeated the process throughout the night, I was worried the floor's concierge would say something. But the transaction had already been made—our money for her acceptance—she ignored us with a professional focus I had only seen in doctors and lawyers on television.

Being the hosts meant we took shots with every new guest that arrived. They'd take a tour and maybe smoke some weed in the closet, or do whatever people were doing in the fogged up walk-in shower. At one point, Soulja Boy came on and a group that had been rehearsing cleared some space and "Cranked Dat," launching into a coordinated dance learned from YouTube. The mythology of *the* end of the year party rose up and buoyed everyone into having a great time. We could've ended the night singing "Kumbaya," it was all so genuine.

And maybe we did. I don't remember. I blacked out before midnight.

The next morning was the familiar Hell of the puking/pack-up/check-out process. The hotel room was a mess to the point where we didn't see any one piece of garbage, just a roiling swarm of trash and filth we weren't cleaning. We left a $50 tip. We hoped any bill would only be in the hundreds, and we'd cover it with the remnants of our betting wins.

To reverse engineer the party's timeline, I corroborated with other guests and checked my saved pictures, rediscovering half-formed memories. Food fights with minibar chocolate. Women up and down the two-story drapes. The Jack and Jill sinks clogged with blood and vomit, respectively. Someone had decided to take a bath in the infinity tub and left with a bathrobe because their clothes were thrown in a trashcan (also filled with puke). One memory burned back to life was my close friend Chris— one of the other hosts— having sex with a dropout-turned-Spearmint Rhino stripper over the blood-filled sink. But that day, I hadn't received any calls from the hotel and thought we got away with throwing the biggest party our class had ever seen.

The mailed invoice from the MGM/Mirage Resorts came with a letter explaining they had been forced to close the room for three days while they repaired it. When I opened the envelope, thick and dangerously unmarked, I couldn't have been prepared. I mentally tried to double-check their list of offenses. Torn drapes (yes), glass in the carpets (sure), broken tile (no idea), and stained marble from the dragon fruit (of course), amongst others. All in the sum of: $5,237.40. My stomach hit my throat. This was what it was like to be caught, for once. My high school world had changed and grown big and dark around me.

I owed the amount to the cardholder listed on the room. Unfortunately, in our desperation to secure a person old enough with a credit card, we made a deal with the Devil. We hadn't used one of our normal betting contacts, who would've had us pay in advance. Instead, I owed $5,300 to a bipolar junkie. Someone who posed a real chance of taking my life. My mother.

She made it clear, in a cold tone, that I was going to pay her every penny by the end of the month or she'd kill me. Most mothers make that threat partially in jest, but I believed her. She wore her mental disorders like badges of honor and thought her addiction to pain pills went unnoticed by those around her. Suffice to say she was temperamental.

She also had means to back up her threat. My step-dad fought her off after she came after me with a hammer when I was twelve, and I later helped her buy him a Glock 17 for

Seat Open

his birthday, and because he was a felon. Most recently, my grandmother had moved out when she caught my mom standing over her with a pillow, about to smother her to death in the middle of the night. My mother was like a one-woman Rob Zombie-directed Addams Family.

Because of the haphazard home life, I spent most of high school as grateful bystander in the dysfunctional homes of my friends. Currently, I was laying low at a friend's house whose parents had bought a Bed N' Breakfast in Oregon and left him with an empty three-bedroom in the Vegas suburbs for an undetermined number of months. Our friend group effectively moved in, drinking and smoking by the pool every night, generally doing whatever we pleased. It was a mix between Animal House and Lord of the Flies. Everyone was Jack, no one was Piggy. It was only surprising it had taken us this long to get in over our heads.

Three hundred in savings, needing five thousand in weeks, meant I required a high leverage return. Fortunately, I had one—Texas Hold' Em.

I had spent my senior year of high school dabbling in low stakes online poker. I learned the game through free online tournaments and had spun up a bankroll from pennies into hundreds of dollars on a few occasions. I had aspirations to be a professional poker player and while that could've been attributed to my gambling-addict father, I chalked it up to loftier ambitions—wanting a lot of money and no responsibility.

One of the few things I brought with me to the Flies house was a VHS copy of the best poker movie ever made—*Rounders*. I rewatched *Rounders* to help me prepare for my run. In the movie, Mike McD needs to win $15,000 from a stake of $1,200. He beats a grizzled Russian named Teddy KGB and pays back a loan from his law professor with enough money to go to Vegas. I had the movie on a loop like it held the magic words to wealth somewhere in its sharp dialogue. "We can't run from who we are. Our destiny chooses us." Surely, this was telling me to gamble for everything I had.

It seemed my plan had two problems—I wasn't 21, so I had nowhere to play and I was broke, so I had nothing to play with.

But like a winged angel, Sarah swept in.

Sarah was one of my best friends. She was also a manager at Starbucks, as close to a corporate job as any of us would probably ever have. She was the glue of stability for our group, frugal with her money, a wellspring of creativity and craft. Upon hearing my predicament, Sarah loaned me $1,000 from her savings as seed money for a poker fund, telling me to pay her back "whenever I could." Sarah believed in underdogs.

I couldn't play cards in Vegas. I had snuck onto tables a few times before, but when I succeeded I was fraught with anxiety, waiting to be caught. For this session, I would need hours of uninterrupted play and couldn't afford to have my stack confiscated.

I turned to California—specifically the Morongo Casino Resort & Spa.

Morongo was one of a half-dozen Indian casinos that catered to the 18+ crowds of San Diego and Orange County. I had never been, but I heard about it on the poker forums. To an 18 year old poker player, it was the proving grounds.

Chris—resident stripper charmer and one of the other hosts—agreed to co-pilot for the potential suicide mission. Armed with Sarah's stake, corner store snacks, and a full tank of gas, Chris and I left from our friend's house at 8AM in his beat-up 2002 Pontiac Grand Prix.

We throttled down the I-5 toward San Diego.

Seat Open

We had no hotel room booked nor money for one, but we had our youthful optimism and we savored that like ten year olds sneaking wine at communion.

I took over driving duties somewhere in Bakersfield. In spans of silence, I used my phone to read from TwoPlusTwo—a popular poker forum. Steady conversation from the best players in the game was invaluable. I read tips on live play—being aware of physical tells or how to scout for a table change—hoping they would pay off later. I crammed as much information as I could into my brain, pouring in more as the rest settled.

The drive was expected to take six hours. By hour seven, Chris and I switched back. It wasn't clear if this was a miscalculation or destiny already working against us. I needed to hop straight to the games, and I'd be overripe from a long car ride. Fortunately, nerves and the sheer terror of my mother kept me alert, focused, and even relatively upbeat. This was all somehow fairly normal.

We were an hour outside of San Diego when I saw a group of lights in the middle of the desert. A tall building— the tallest for miles— with sleek, curved sides standing erect. It looked like a leftover child's toy in a sandbox, emanating brilliant, purple light into the surrounding barren darkness.

We pulled in and tucked our car into a corner of the fourth floor parking garage in preparation of needing to covertly sleep there.

We navigated through the casino to the poker room. A mix of the typical desperate coked-out energy tempered with the reserved atmosphere of a home game—it felt like the perfect setting for my personal third act. I was ready to prove my worth as a poker player.

I asked Chris what he would do in the time it took me to make the money back. He planned on using $100 to buy

Blockhead

into the lowest stakes table to try and tap into his own reservoir of luck. Chris volunteered donating his winnings, which I thought was incredibly generous. While my friends did what they could to alleviate the debt, we had essentially gambled to pay for the room in the first place, and I hadn't expected much help to come from them.

I asked for a seat in the lone $2/$5 game running and was directed to the table in the back. In every poker room, there was a natural gravitas around the highest stakes game. Morongo was no different. Two massage girls worked on different players. This was the pro's corner. I bought in $500 and eyed the stacks. In front of every player—all heavy set men—were more chips than I had ever had in my bankroll at any one time. There were thousands on the table. The game was "deep." This is where I could be a hero.

The Dealer asked me for my ID and noted the fact I was a new player, having turned 18 only a few months prior. I didn't mention my savviness derived from PokerStars.com, wanting to keep the other players in the dark. That was the advice from the message boards, at least.

I had to sit out and focus on stacking my chips for the first orbit of cards, because my hands were shaking so badly anything else would have been a dead giveaway to my nerves. There were other moments when it was clear I was still new to a live poker table. I peeled up my cards to reveal a good hand—Ace and Jack—and while I was staring, thinking, calculating exactly how much I could win, I was tapped and quickly realized that the entire table was waiting on me. I folded my cards, silently berating myself. This happened a few times, and once I made myself fold a premium hand because of it.

Despite these speed bumps, I immediately ran up my stack to $1,000. I was getting good cards and playing

Seat Open

aggressively. At this rate, I'd be able to hit our dollar goal in a day or two.

While I shuffled chips and thought of the money I needed to win, the shadow loomed large over me. Staring over the edge of the cliff of debt was all it took, I started bleeding chips.

Every pot I lost widened the chasm between what I had and what I needed. I was getting the hang of live poker play, but not fast enough. I hit a streak where I was "card dead"— nothing but bad, unplayable hands—the worst thing possible, next to losing.

My stack kept dwindling. The hours passed. My play worsened. High-stakes poker is a game of mental discipline, the brand which an eighteen year-old almost certainly lacks.

I had foolishly thought I could mitigate luck with talent. My plan required me to be constantly getting good cards and constantly winning with them. My dreams of success slowly twisted, and I picked up on the debased degeneracy I was actually taking part in. Gambling to pay a debt.

I shook my head; the negative self-talk in poker, I was well versed in. I left my stack and took a break from the table. I checked in on Chris. We'd been there over six hours and had settled into a grind. He was down to his last $40 and hoped to explore the cafeteria soon. Things were not going well for us.

I went to the bathroom. I sat in a stall at the end of the row and closed my eyes in the quiet, cool room. Bathrooms have always been a sacred place for me in the casino. Obvious joking aside, it's the only place in the casino where you have any privacy, even if it's a few feet in any direction. I thought this was a secret of mine until it came up with some pro poker friends years later— they all treasured bathrooms in the same way.

9

With my eyes closed, I felt like I could be anywhere in the world, and I didn't have to be there, then. Perhaps there was an internet thread for how to deal with an existential poker crisis. I read TwoPlusTwo posts on my phone. I scrolled past an article about a 19 year old winning $900k in Australia that made me boil with jealousy and stopped on—

Gamble, Gamble – the God of Gambling

This could be useful. I opened it.
The original poster had written a small paragraph detailing the myth of "Gamble Gamble." Gamble Gamble, according to legend, was the invisible God of Luck living inside every poker room. A bastardized version of the Goddess Fortuna, he was an impish goblin who could be summoned by a player to turn the tides of chance. It was alleged Gamble Gamble could switch out cards as they were being dealt. I remembered many times I heard players say "gamble, gamble" when they were all-in. I thought it was just an expression, but now I understood.
They were summoning a degenerate demon king to pass its judgment—who in my mind was dripping in fine silk and jewels. What I pictured wasn't dissimilar from a Saturday morning cartoon villain.
I thought about my mother waiting for her money. I remembered I had work to do. I went back to the poker room with a new god to pray to. Chris had lost his last $40 and gone to sleep off casino dinner in the car. There were no more familiar faces in the room. It felt like every table had been recast.

Seven hours in, the table had finally shifted into what I was hoping for—louder players, more opportunities. Our game, despite its relatively tame $500 buy-in, was one of the highest stakes games running in 150 miles. It was the

Seat Open

weekend, so rich professionals and kids with trust funds had packed into the poker room. The tables were lively, mine especially. I had everything I needed.

The night grew later and my nerves grew thinner. My heart skipped a beat as I picked up two eights. Finally, a decent hand. The pot was raised to $30 pre-flop with multiple callers. Two thick-handed Italian men mirrored the brick-like Russians I sat between. Did they have great cards? Speculative hands worse than mine? I had no idea. But the flop brought out an 8. I thanked Gamble Gamble and prayed no one noticed how nervous I was, manically shuffling my chips. Had someone seen me move in my seat? Had I moved?

I slid out a stack of red chips—$80. I was called by one player. This was almost 2% toward my goal. The turn paired the board, giving me a full house. Did he have four of a kind? Maybe he had a better full house. No, this was where I built my stack. I bet $220. Way too much. I had dollar signs for eyes.

The large Italian stared me down. I could tell he wanted to call, but that he knew better. I didn't know how to convince him one way or the other. I stared at a single spot on the table until my eyes watered.

Finally, he asked. "If I fold, will you show?"

I said nothing. He folded.

"Let me see."

I thought about showing him my hand. It could ingratiate him to me, force him to fold when I was bluffing later in the night. Instead I mucked my cards, sliding them face down to the dealer.

The Russian next to me, who had been silent the whole night, spoke up. "Good job."

I looked at him.

"Don't ever give them anything for free," he said.

He flashed me what he must've thought was a smile. I knew this was one of the lessons at the poker table that I would remember long after I finished playing. He was like a television version of *Rounders*' Teddy KGB. I felt like Big Bird on Sesame Street.

    I took a walk to stretch my legs. Chris was wandering the casino on the phone to his girlfriend back in Vegas. I grabbed the car keys from him and went back to the garage. I counted my roll: $1,100. Up a little bit, including expenses. I barely registered frustration. Frankly, I wanted to go back to the table, but knew I should get some rest. I had a blinding headache and was dehydrated. Sleep would have to solve both. The windows were tinted dark for Las Vegas summer. Now, they provided the perfect cover from security guards. I took my car nap.

    I woke up from a dream of a few years before, when my mom threw me headfirst into a bureau. My skull ached and I wasn't sure if my pain was from the impact or the memory. Regardless, I was awake. I went back in to the poker room, bringing my entire bankroll. I worked hard on visualizing myself winning. Escaping my mother's wrath. I would make it happen. I wanted to pray to Gamble Gamble, but I wasn't sure if he was reachable outside of the poker room. I hoped he had a soft spot for players under the age of 21.

    I sat down at a new table, but as I played, I couldn't find a flow. I whittled down my stack, calling raises with good cards, only to see them turn to napkins. Occasionally, I was allowed to win a tiny pot. My brain was working against me by this point. The time in between hands felt more painful and drawn out than the hands themselves. I was in tailspin. A slow, confusing death. This was very poor visualization.

    Fatigue worsened and the chips stopped looking like bets and started looking like money again. That wasn't a "preflop raise," it was twenty dollars. I found myself in a

Seat Open

large pot, but I didn't remember how I got in. I had a pair of sevens. There was another seven on the board for three of a kind, but I didn't feel good. There were two other players, already all-in. The board was incredibly "connected," meaning a large combination of cards gave them good odds at winning. They likely had very good hands, too. We'd be gambling for the ~$1500 pot.

But that's what I was there to do. I called and we rolled over our hands. A straight draw and a flush draw.

"Gamble, gamble," I said, not sure if I was doing it right.

Another spade came. The board didn't pair. I lost the monster pot to a flush.

A young, hoodied pro won, dragging the chips in. He allowed himself a small smile, possibly on his own redemptive quest, much better prepared than me. I shamefully stuck my hand in my pocket and pulled what was left of the roll out—about $400.

I bought in for the rest. It was 7AM.

Chris sat behind me at an empty table trying not to fall asleep, lest he be asked by the floor man to leave. I thought that was ridiculous. We couldn't possibly be the only ones living there that night.

I picked up pocket Kings and re-raised an old, rich player there to "have fun" aka lose money. He shoved all-in for more chips than I had. I snap-called and hoped for the best. He had Ace-Jack. I was well ahead. But an Ace on the flop put me behind. No other kings came out and I lost another massive hand. I checked my pocket already knowing the scary truth— I had no more money.

I was shocked. I sat dumbly in my chair, in front of the empty space of felt where my stack once was, but was now being slid to someone else.

I turned to Chris and muttered, "Let's go."

Our pockets were empty. We were defeated.

Blockhead

Back on the road, I felt gutted. Despaired. I leaned deep into the passenger seat, feeling the weight of the world, or at least another $1,000 in debt. I had no idea what to do. The warning strip buzzed underneath me.

I looked at Chris, who shook awake.

"Sorry," he managed, literally wiping drool from his chin. Part of me considered letting him drive. It would've made things a lot easier.

We pulled over, and I took the wheel. But the hum of the car worked its magic on me, and soon I was falling asleep, too. I blinked and opened my eyes 100 ft. down the road. The terror only worked to keep me awake in bursts, but I already knew I was unlucky. We wouldn't get any breaks. My nerve had been broken. I saw an exit for a shopping mall and took it. I pulled into a Jack in the Box parking lot, away from any buildings. Chris was snoring in the passenger seat. The inside of the car was still cold from a night in the desert. I put my hoodie up and let sleep take over.

I woke up feeling like my throat was closing. The inside of the car was fogged and I was drenched in sweat. Baking under the California sun in an open lot, it turned out, was a bad idea. Chris was dead to the world, though I was pretty sure still technically alive. I threw open the car door and cool morning air rushed in.

The sensation sent shivers down my spine. For the first time all trip, I felt pure relief thinking we wouldn't die, and I lost consciousness with one foot out the open car door. Someone could've robbed us, if we had anything worth taking.

Chris woke in a coughing fit, suddenly affected by the heat, shortly after 10AM.

"What the fuck."

Seat Open

He sat up choking, puked out the car door, and shook it off. The commotion woke me up and instantly we were ready. The mood was unexpectedly high. If you can survive poverty, you can survive anything. Even more poverty.

We picked up food at Jack in the Box and ate in the car, getting something other than candy and beef jerky in our stomachs before the long drive home. I texted my friends and told them about my defeat. They consoled me, and I consoled myself. My narrative had taken a turn— I wouldn't be coming home the hero. There would be no fanfare. This wasn't *Rounders*.

Chris and I pulled up to our friend's house. We'd be staying there through the rest of the summer, but I didn't want to go in. I didn't want any of it.

I snuck into the house through a side door directly into the spare room I had been staying in. I didn't want to see anyone. I wasn't ready to be recognized as a loser.

I emptied my backpack. Everything smelled like cigarettes. I touched something hard and plastic on my floor. The VHS copy of *Rounders*. I threw it against the wall. It cracked in half. I picked up the broken husk and smashed it again. My friends called my name from outside asking if I was okay. I stomped on the pieces like ants. I felt them crunch.

To pay back my mother, I sold my car. That was the only card left to play, so I played it. I paid back Sarah over the next 8 months, grinding from pennies in online poker. My "pipe dream" of playing online and building a bankroll turned out to be the best plan. I could've let myself be discouraged by my embarrassing spectacle of failure, but I looked at it the other way. This was only the beginning. I couldn't fall any lower. I could only go up. I had been blessed by Gamble Gamble. Baptized as a poker player.

Seat Open

I met Mike Neel in my sophomore year of high school. We sat next to each other in the back of Geography Honors. He let me tell most of the jokes even though he was funnier.

Mike Neel and I were periphery friends, enjoying each other's wit. Mike Neel had the type of name that had to be spoken in full, and he appreciated my opinion on this. He had even been at the famed "hotel party" our senior year. But our friendship didn't start blossoming off school grounds until freshman year of college. We both went to UNLV, affectionately termed University of Never Leaving Vegas. This was shortly after my Morongo trip, when I had the eagerness beaten out of me, and was forced to learn patience at the nickel-and-dime games offered on AbsolutePoker.com. I grew my third $50 deposit into a few hundred dollars and coupled with a steady win-rate, even at terribly low stakes, planted a seed of confidence that made me continue the grind.

At a typically claustrophobic college party held by a mutual friend, Mike Neel approached me with a glint in his eye. He said he heard I "played five ten" which we both understood meant high stakes—five dollar, ten dollar— and would've put me worlds away from holding my Bud Light at a freshman apartment party. I explained that "five ten" meant five-cent, ten-cent online. Mike Neel gave a laugh of relief.

He told me he was playing the same stakes on Full Tilt Poker. At first, I was slightly threatened to know the identity of another anonymous online warrior. But Mike was so eager to talk about the game that I was swept up in having a comrade and didn't have time to consider a competitor.

Seat Open

Mike and I continued into Facebook messages about poker tracking software and hand histories. We felt about even in terms of skill, and quickly started texting each other about every questionable poker spot. When to raise, what stakes we wanted to play, how to handle other regulars— we discussed it all and our friendship grew parallel to our obsession with the game.

I had classes on Monday, Wednesday, and Friday. Those days I drove to campus and met up with Mike Neel on the top floor of the UNLV library. From any of the tables, you could see the tail end of the Strip, an empty lot, and a UNLV science research building. We set up our laptops across from each other at one of the study tables like we were playing a game of Battleship. In any complex or confusing hands, we could immediately ask the other for advice. Schoolwork was an afterthought.

We balanced fifteen tables on our respective sites, battling with anonymous avatars like MrSoros, fishinU, and cy00. We spent hours reviewing hands in PokerTracker, trying to find weaknesses in our games. We picked up deficiencies in each other's playstyles and grew to adapt. We were rhino and oxpecker both.

We warred against the other players, throwing off-hand comments like we were on ESPN, bullshitting over our chip stacks. It beat the isolating feeling of playing online alone. During one of our library sessions, I sat two tables with a player named "GONZOBRKLYN." He was immediately notable for having the twin tendencies of an ideal recreational player; he didn't care what his cards were, and he didn't care how much he put in the middle. This was the kind of player who could make your month.

But Gonzo was being "hit by the deck," meaning he couldn't lose. Gonzo raised when I didn't have cards and always had something better when I made a hand. He turned over impossibly-conceived straights, bizarre two-pairs, or the worst; we would get all our chips in and he'd

Blockhead

show a total bluff, only to have the turn and river save him, channeling a good hand from the divine. I had moved up in stakes, which allowed me to lose $900 to Gonzo in about 45 minutes. A manageable sum, but at the time it felt like an insurmountable debt, an enormous loss.

Gonzo sat out from our tables and disappeared, taking what used to be my money with him. Mike had been watching and could only offer distant words of consolation. "Damn savages."

I did the math. I could've burned $10 a minute for the whole hour and lost less money. Devoid of all calm, I threw my wireless mouse down an aisle of books about Marine Biology. Then, I went and shamefully collected it. What else was I supposed to do? Mike Neel watched in silence, understanding.

Mike Neel had an affinity for Civil War general William Tecumseh Sherman. He approached poker with the same ethos Sherman approached the battlefield with: burn it all. While I resented the other regulars, finding infinitesimal ways to loathe them, Mike only understood them. His mastery came from his empathy. In his eyes, we were all coworkers, clocking in and out together, working for a naturally divisive goal. Mike was always upset I played a little loose. Why not wait for more advanced weaponry when going to war?

Mike's poker work ethic was strong. He managed his bankroll well and was always trying to improve. I would frequently check my phone and see texts like, "Folded JQs UTG feel like a real live poker player!" I knew he was clicking away, stacking digital chips. He was in the middle of accumulating a "Full Tilt Points card" which allowed him to use his player points as money via a mail-order debit card. For grinders like us, it was a godsend.

We played online fourteen hours, every day, usually ending our sessions rendezvousing at Roberto's Taco Shop

Seat Open

to go over hands and get in requisite social contact. We sat at the back tables eating bean and cheese burritos dripping with grease, going over the day's opponents, plotting our takeover of the Las Vegas Strip.

Then, Black Friday happened.

I was always an early riser and usually found myself at the tables catching the after-work European rush at 8am Vegas-time. I checked the poker forums waiting for games to start, and it was shaping up to be an unforgettable day when I saw a thread about a poker site replaced with a new homepage—

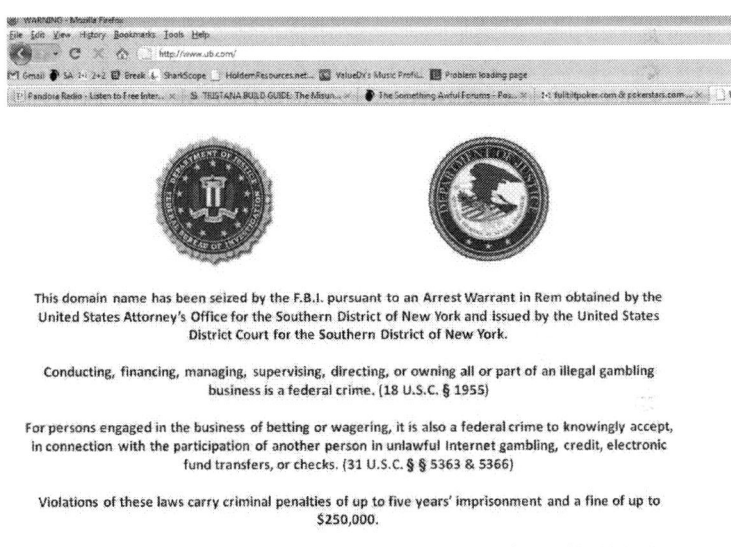

Poker players spent the next few days and nights circulating around what little information we had. It was a depressing game of Telephone, passing back and forth the same facts in hopes of generating more. Players sold off their balances for pennies on the dollar. Cash-rich pros bailed out others too young to have known better. Stories of $500 in the bank and $50,000 stuck on Full Tilt became common and condolences were doled. After five days, an official press release came out.

The Department of Justice shut down the three largest online poker sites: PokerStars, Full Tilt, and Absolute Poker. Worse, Full Tilt had essentially been operating as a Ponzi scheme. Our funds were not only locked away by the government in perpetuity, but were also nonexistent. Bad luck had hit in ways we didn't know were possible.

In retrospect, the shutdown should not have come as a surprise. The sites had started increasing the frequency of giveaways to generate quick revenue for themselves. Players knew the stance of the federal government, though it had mostly devolved to "don't ask, don't tell." Poker was rife with subpar morality. The narrative that ten top poker players got together and formed Full Tilt Poker into a billion dollar organization sounded ludicrous because it was. None of this changed the fact that an entire population of fiercely smart 20-somethings were now out of the job.

Within weeks, players were moving to Canada and Mexico. Websites sprung up overnight to help poker pros relocate, continuing the lifestyle of convenience we were used to with an agency that arranged visas, housing, and most importantly, streamlined the process of registering on the international poker sites.

But Mike and I stayed in Las Vegas. We didn't play high enough to justify dropping out of college and uprooting our lives, plus the outlook for online games was bleak if not provably hazardous. I had been managing weekly cash-outs, but Mike had kept his entire bankroll on Full Tilt for sake of liquidity and was badly burned. We needed a new income stream, fast. Fortunately, this was a simple transition—a change in our commute.

If there was a silver lining of the DOJ poker shutdown, it was the timing; Mike and I had just turned 21 only months apart. Instead of staying in our bedrooms, we could

Seat Open

now drive thirty minutes to the Las Vegas Strip where twenty-plus poker rooms ran dozens of tables every hour of the day. While I had played some live poker before, I could hardly classify my weekend binge gambling at Morongo as live poker experience. But how hard could live games be after spending so much time online? Didn't pilots learn on flight simulators?

We stalked the forums to find low stakes games for our transition to live play. We didn't have much buffer to spend as "poker tuition" to learn the finer differences of the game and needed a teaching hospital—a battlefield made of the soft, spongey turf from a school playground. Enter the Beginner Game.

Mike once described the Beginner Game as a money factory with free drinks. In details, he recalled it as "whooping and hollering, club music, casino chaos, and perhaps the most solid looking bunch of tight poker players I've ever seen."

The MGM Grand ran the lowest stakes game in town—a single table of 50-cent, 1-dollar blinds with a $50 max buy-in. The first time I played, even though my hands were shaking, I couldn't help but smile at the fact that a Kennedy piece was being bet, stacked, coveted in an actual casino outside of 1974. It felt like a home game, except for the smoke-stained felt and the escorts perched at the bar next door. It was equal parts serendipitous and pitiful. Mike and I had found a new home.

Due to the impoverished amounts at play, no one at the game was a very good player. There were moments of actual talent, but mostly it was bored degenerates unable to put together a larger buy-in, tourists who wanted to lose the minimum, and a cast of sad regulars, including us.

There was Vinny—a fast-talking, skeletal hustler with a silver tooth in his bottom jaw that made you think he was always conning you. Vinny once told us he was wanted in the state of New York, then pulled up the warrant online to prove it. He said he was trying to make a run at pro gambling—poker and sports. He paid $100 a week to sleep on a hooker's couch walking distance from the MGM.

Vinny was the closest thing we had to a friendly upperclassman. One night, Vinny—the consummate tight player—got his big stack in against my big stack and already made hand. He got lucky and spiked one of his few outs. I was stunned. This was my first sense of understanding the strict distinction between friends and money. I wasn't sure whether to feel happy for Vinny or sad for me, but I felt something between annoyed and confused and I had to feel it then, in front of him. I almost felt a bit betrayed.

"Sorry about that. I didn't think you had it," Vinny said. He offered to buy me a bagel and schmear at the neighboring deli, which was more of a refund than I deserved.

The regulars were mostly sad, silent and grey-skinned. Several borderline homeless. Layered in thin fleeces, free casino hoodies, or otherwise glaring signs of a crushed soul. Another New York hustler who barely spoke above a whisper sat next to Vinny one night and told a story, in great detail, of his arrest for a bank robbery in broad daylight. I played against a homeless man who kept all of his belongings in a plastic bag. He bought into the game with bills that smelled like urine. I won his money and spent it on Roberto's with Mike. The Las Vegas version of eating what you kill.

Almost as familiar as the regulars were the dealers. Each with only their nametag to claim their entire identity. Mitch, Toldeo, OH and Grace, Jacksonville, FL. Some of the dealers, like Hank, I'd see more than my own mother.

Hank was tall with a long neck and not much hair. He had the feel of an old Western preacher. That made him oddly fitting as a poker dealer. Hank frequently accused

Seat Open

Mike and me of being related. He could see past the dark hair and glasses, but not through the different ethnicities. "C'mon. You guys are cousins, right?" We gave Hank a new story every night, stoking the comradery between player and dealer, honing our performances.

Mike Neel and I carpooled to the MGM Grand almost every day. I'd drive to his house and he'd drive us down Flamingo. We'd walk the long, freezing cold hallway between the parking garage and the casino with photo booths and $15 bags of caramel popcorn, trying to keep each other's spirits warm with jokes.

The Beginner Game would be the education we needed to the world of poker—which is to say the real world. Mike Neel and I learned lessons on international business when a drunk Indian man sat down at our table to play what he thought was blackjack. He quickly lost $300 and expressed interest in playing more but stood up to leave. We asked why and he explained— he only had rupees in his wallet, unconverted from back home. Having just seen him lose a night's work, Mike and I offered to convert his money at the table, for dollars in our pockets. We could go to a bank and exchange them back any other time, but if he left now, that money was gone forever. The Indian man was humored, but mostly thankful for the convenience. We exchanged a few hundred more and won most of it back, $50 at a time. Some lessons were less obvious.

Fox was another friendly dealer, constantly amused in the simplest ways. He saw everything but what was right in front of him. A deeply profound man with similarities to a Muppet.

Fox had stumbled into a relationship with one of the massage therapists and one night, deep into a session at 5 AM, I asked him how it was going. Fox lost himself in thought for a moment, something on his mind too big to handle.

Blockhead

He stopped dealing which was fine because at that point we mostly didn't care if we were playing. It was only me, Mike, Vinny, and a few other regs. Fox asked our table, "What's the most important decision a man can make in his life?"

Like most tables, ours was entirely male. We thought about it. Looked at each other, hoping someone knew this one.

"Who he marries," someone guessed.

"No," Fox shook that off. "He can change that."

More of us ventured guesses.

"Where he works."

"Where he lives."

"If he has kids or not," I suggested.

"He can change all those," Fox looked at me. Mike and the rest of the table waited for an answer.

"The most important decision in a man's life is who the mother of his children is, because he can never change that."

Mike and I looked at each other with a familiar shared look of shock. Face deadpan, eyes slightly bulged, like a horrified butler. Mike let out a laugh. I was struck with the same realization that came with the answer to a brain teaser. The ringing of truth. I vowed to never forget what Fox told us, whether he was right or not, which he almost certainly wasn't.

Regardless of any given night's lesson, Mike and I usually ended up at the Orleans at 6 AM for a $5 Steak and Eggs special where at least 20% of the other patrons were homeless. It made the Beginner Game look like a meeting of the Young Republicans. It wasn't uncommon to see a family of quiet European tourists burdened with oversized American portions at one table and a man wearing a poncho falling asleep into his soup at another. Sometimes Mike and I invited friends from school to meet us in the

Seat Open

mornings, if their graveyard shifts intersected with ours. Rarely did anyone come twice.

To break up the sedentary lifestyle—driving to the casino to play ten hours and driving back home to eat, sleep, and get high—we added an element of physical activity into our lives. Mike Neel loved baseball and his passion was so infectious that it made me love it, too. His attraction was tied to the narratives in the game. I wasn't watching sports; I was watching beautiful, human tragedies play out under the field lights. We watched baseball while we played poker, battled in a fantasy league, talked about it on our drives home from the Strip.

We even tried playing. But lacking anything more than a love for the game, including a drop of skill, and wanting to keep our gambling schedule, we only managed to get the two of us to show up for "game time," usually scheduled with no advanced notice.

It didn't matter. We'd take turns with one of us batting to the other, standing in the outfield behind 2nd base. Sometimes there'd even be a chance of actually fielding a hit. When we got really ambitious, the fielder would move in and play pitcher. Form over flash. We took heart in the simple action of putting ourselves out on the dirt; in the early mornings, sometimes after a poker session, leaving before it got unbearably hot at 8am.

After a few months, we were making more than we were losing and wanted to move up in stakes. We had come to the Beginner Game months before, unsure how to stack chips, and while we weren't yet seasoned pros, it was time to leave the nest.

We checked out the $1 - $2 games across the city. The next step. We tested the waters in every room around town, settling at first on a local's spot closer to home—the Red Rock. We were drawn by a twelve minute drive, door-to-door. Maybe it was something in the water, or the massive "bad beat jackpot" that drew all kinds of skeezy Las Vegas locals, but sessions at the Red Rock were generally strange.

One of our first nights there, Mike and I met Nick S. and Steve S.. They immediately came across as alternate reality versions of us. Versions that had gone to better high schools, had relationships with their parents, and didn't do drugs. They even went to UNLV, too. The connection gave our dual lives another layer. We needed to remember inside jokes outside contexts. Mike and I barely spoke to them farther than a "See you at the library" on the way to the cashier.

Mike and I had picked up the habit, every time we cashed out, of grabbing a few rubber bands for our wrists. If I won more money than I expected, I used them as a makeshift money clip. If I lost, I gave myself snaps as a simpleton learning mechanism. Mike Neel and I utilized the system often. Over the next few years playing together, if he was Sherman, I was his Grant in all but rank. He was the melancholic and I was the alcoholic, but we had each other's backs through thick and thin.

Early in the Red Rock transition, Mike and I played against a dentist. He lived on the nearby country club, a pleasant, plump Bengali man. The $1 - $2 game had much more money on the table than our $50 buy-in roots, but the dentist had brought thousands and he wanted to lose. Correction— he just wanted to have fun. Fortunately for us, he chose to unwind decades of discipline studying teeth by playing incredibly passive poker.

In these situations, the better player wins...unless luck plays a factor. And like GONZOBRKLYN a few years prior, the dentist had my number. Every time I turned over a made hand, he turned over trash and the deck bailed him out. *This was what I wanted*, I told myself, sending another stack of chips his way. He had to get lucky. I was getting my chips in as a massive favorite. That was the goal. I was

Seat Open

performing well as a poker player. My heart was racing, and I had a hurried feeling in my stomach and eyes.

I was down to my last buy-in when Mike went on a heater. There was a large, three-way pot where I was in with the best hand versus Mike and the dentist. Mike ended up getting lucky, taking most of the table's chips, and all of the dentist's stack. The dentist left and shortly after, with no reason to be there, we left too. I was on the tail-end of a two month downswing and losing hurt. What was worse was the unspoken schadenfreude between Mike and I in the car. Any congratulations rang hollow. Any consolation was disingenuous. We sat in the parking lot of the Red Rock in silence. It was early, only 3AM.

"How do you feel about a pit stop at Wal-Mart?"

Mike Neel had been talking about buying the latest PlayStation for weeks and had now met his goal with what I still felt was my money. I hadn't expected us to go that night, while I was still reeling from my losses. It was like salt in the wound but he was my best friend, and if I was being honest, I had my own wish list. I couldn't help but be willing to go with Mike. Spending so much time together, even me losing, him winning felt like we both won. Anyway, he was driving.

Over the next few months, we explored other poker rooms in the Strip and settled at the Bellagio.

The $1 - $3 games had manageable buy-ins ($300), were full of tourists, had no jackpot drop, and with the North Valet feet away, allowed for a tight twenty-minute commute. Half the time though, we braved Las Vegas Blvd and its endless right turn lane into the Bellagio garage to park on the top floor. From the edge of the deck, the Las Vegas Strip shined down in a brilliant panorama with the miniature Eiffel Tower, a 50 ft. Britney Spears ad, and the hotel behemoths of the Strip, our equivalent of religious temples or the holy capital. The Bellagio parking garage was the best view in town.

"The B," a nickname we used as often as we could, applying some put-on road gambler sheen, became our home base. There were days on end where at least one of us was always in the poker room, grinding away. It was at the Bellagio that Mike put in his first thirty hour session. I had a childhood friend whose mom was a poker dealer there. For months, I never saw him, only checking in through his mother. Despite being quite a gambler herself, she felt obligated to give more than one maternal warning. I felt obligated to tip twice as much.

We tried out the Venetian and the Wynn. While the Bellagio was the go-to room in the poker community, we craved diversity of experience believing it would help our game.

One night at the Wynn, in their deep $1-$2 game, Mike Neel and I made close to $1,000 each. We cashed out after the four hour session feeling like kings. This was exactly the feeling we sought—earning our keep and almost feeling like we got away with more than we deserved. On the way out, we eyed the $2-$5 game. It was the next rung in the ladder to high stakes success. There were two seats open.

One of the regulars, who I had seen before and knew as a successful tournament pro— featured several times on ESPN brooding for the cameras— saw us window shopping and waved us over. Foolishly, we humored him.

"Seat open," he called out, almost like a challenge. We still had our wads of 100s in our hands.

Mike Neel, always more clever than me and feeling bolstered by the win, engaged the pro. "I don't know," Mike's voice broadcast uncertainty. He was an actor and used that to his strength in the poker room. "Haven't I seen you on TV before?" He was pulling the guy's chain, perfectly.

Seat Open

But without missing a beat, the pro shot back. "Yeah, COPS."

There was something so deft about his comeback that neither of us could say anything. We only smiled and nodded, and he went back to his game, knowing full well that in the strength of his rebuke, he snuffed out any chance of our playing there. We went back to the parking garage feeling much less victorious, tails between our legs. We weren't yet them.

We eventually took our shots at the $2 - $5, filled with venerated regulars for whom their drink order— "green tea, paper cup"—were lifestyles. There were many more players who showed up at the same time, spoke to each other with first names instead of seat numbers, asked about the family. But our expenses started rising, our win rates stagnated, and our bankrolls need constant trimming and thus, constant infusing.

On the poker forum that had served as the backdrop for our shared social network, we met a poster named "Sharky221." As we'd later learn, Sharky was one of many Southerners who loved beer and football. Sharky could always be found in the bleachers of his local high school football game. And he graciously shared his love for Southern football in the form of sports betting picks.

Anyone who has spent twenty minutes at a poker table has heard of someone's alleged knowledge of a certain player, sport, or game promising riches at the book. So in September, when Mike and I found Sharky's thread titled "SEC FOOTBALL LIVE JOURNAL" tucked away in a subforum, we were skeptical. But after two weeks, Sharky had only picked winners. 6-0 against the spread. How long could this go on?

Mike and I quickly partitioned our bankrolls. Following somewhat strict betting guidelines, we followed Sharky's picks through the promised land of SEC football. Sharky started including confidence levels. Sure enough, his 3 unit picks were "only" 75% winners, but his 5 unit picks, halfway through the season, were 9-0. Sharky was King Midas.

We replaced hours normally spent at the poker table making trips to the sportsbook, checking lines, signing up for bonus money we knew Sharky would turn into cash. The income felt passive, like collecting rent on a building we owned but never had to visit.

The college football national championship that year was between, blessedly, two SEC teams Sharky had been winning on all year—Alabama and LSU. Sharky had 5-unit plays on the total and spread. We bet heavy and won both. Our only regret was that we didn't bet more. But the golden goose Mike Neel and I found was just as suddenly migrating farther South.

Sharky, by this point, had created a brand for himself and had a friend—Jsharp55—hop on as a "college basketball sharp." Mike and I cautiously bet a few of his picks until it was determined he was just another mortal, like the rest of us, and we quickly moved on. I took this moment to consider my future.

I didn't want to be gambling forever. I had become friends with some very successful players and seen that, while I was good at the game, I wasn't great. A $45/hr expectation at $2-$5 was nice, but as a poker player, there's nothing bigger than the stack in front of you. No pension other than a bad beat jackpot, a life based on luck instead of hope. It seemed most poker players were pivoting into two fields: investment banking or law. I hated math, so I chose law.

I left for law school, leaving Mike to grind the felt tables alone while he got his ducks in a row to head to Los Angeles to be an actor. He told me he was optimistic and that, while he wouldn't be cast as a leading man, his appeal as a roguish Buddy Holly would get him gigs. I wished him luck, saying Hollywood was full of vipers and children. He made do in the creative muck that was the Las Vegas arts scene in the meanwhile.

I visited Vegas and Mike often. We checked up on our old Roberto's table, our world takeover plans still being executed at a snail's pace.

I kept playing poker, betting sports, and gambling generally. Mike took his shots at the snakepit of low stakes locals poker tournaments, as tough a field as any to find success. He took odd jobs, never shirking the poker player mentality. Not while working a sketchy beauty cream kiosk at Planet Hollywood's Miracle Mile. Not while delivering subs for Quizno's. He always had a plan. Every new hustle he treated like the first, like cards.

Mike went unappreciated by the illiterate natives of Las Vegas. He auditioned for a local commercial. A company was shooting an ad for new World Series of Poker software—not to be played for real money, but still, online poker back in some form. Times were a-changing. I told Mike he was a lock to get the role. A former poker player turned actor auditioning as an online poker player. It was the acting version of pocket aces.

Mike didn't get the role.

Mike was a poker dealer for a while, wanting to stay close to the action. He even dealt cash games at the WSOP. Though I visited several times, I never had him deal to me. There would have been something fundamentally unsound about both of us being at the table but not playing next to each other.

One of the last texts Mike Neel sent me was asking, "What was that line Fox the Dealer told us?"

I didn't have to think at all. "The most important decision a man can make is who the mother of his children is. Because it can never change."

Blockhead

Text bubbles, followed by Mike's response: "Then I wonder what the second most important decision is. Because we have a lot of time between then and now."

Three months later, I was at my birthday dinner with my law school girlfriend. A night on the town in Chicago. I wondered why I hadn't received a text from Mike Neel all day. I didn't mind. Birthdays didn't matter to us. Then, one of my closest friends Sarah, asked me if I had seen Mike's Facebook page. His wall had been transformed into a digital moratorium.

> RIP
> Bro, I can't believe this is real.
> RIP Mike.

I blinked processing the information. I'd later find out Mike Neel killed himself.

I had two choices: react to the news, and though I didn't care about the dinner, ruin the night for my anxious girlfriend who worked hard at putting everything together. Or, put on a poker face. Sit through dinner. Through churros. Smile with no teeth at my birthday candles. Ride the train home with her falling asleep next to me and pretend to wake up to the news the next morning. Then I'd say *That's horrible,* and much later, *but at least last night was nice.* This was a plan Mike Neel would've understood. He would've appreciated the performance.

I didn't go to Mike Neel's funeral. Instead, I stayed at law school, an emotional wreck, for on-campus interviews. Normally high pressure, I felt nothing but rage I tried not to feel. I heard enough from Mike's only human ex-girlfriend about the service to tell me I would've hated it. She told me one woman wept on the lectern because, while her and Mike's bond was recent, she said she knew it was

Seat Open

incredibly strong, and she knew him better than anyone "toward the end." I deleted his messages to me about her.

Looking back through our conversation, there were flags that could've been seen as signs.

"Allies are in Berlin," I texted one night, after a particularly devastating session, to which he responded, "I'll go get Eva and the gasoline drum." A memory driving home after a long night and me threatening to take us into a light pole. I asked him if I should. He told me not to joke.

It took me a while to address the pain over Mike Neel's suicide. My anger over not being able to tell him that in the big picture, poker was the beginner game. I was an only child from a family of addicts, with no one at home I could look in the eyes. Mike was the only person I ever learned to trust. It wasn't an invisible trust assigned at birth to strangers. It was trust built over years of watching each other's stacks on break, putting in each other's sports bets, giving consolation over bad luck, or pretending to not notice me crying on the ride back home.

A few years later, I was showing the city to a new girlfriend. She understood what Mike's loss meant, she had loss of her own. I slipped out to the MGM's poker room.

The Beginner Game was long gone, as I had heard, but I took a seat at another game and stared at blue one-dollar chips, stamped with the familiar MGM lion heads, wondering foolishly if any were the same chips that Mike Neel and I used so many years ago. I pocketed one, desperate to hold some concrete piece of the past.

I was shocked when a taller, thinner Hank sat down across from me. He looked so much older than I remembered. He greeted me like an old friend, though I wasn't sure he recognized me. Then, he stunned me and asked, "Where's your brother?"

After all these years, Mike Neel and I were still playing together in his memories. I told him he wasn't there right

Blockhead

now, but he'd be back. Then I went to the bathroom and cried my eyes out.

Chicago Bulls

In 2012, I was a first-year law student in Illinois which meant that I was at a Presidential Election Party on November 6th. I might have watched the coverage as I normally did, stoned in my apartment, but that year I had a vested interest. I had bet my law school tuition on Barack Obama.

I picked my law school for the generous scholarship they offered, based on some combination of LSAT score and my parents' racial makeup. They apparently didn't care much about the detailed personal statement I wrote about my mother's murder attempts, just that she was Mexican. Growing up poor, I was smart enough to shut up and take the money.

The first months of law school were un-exciting. The constant repetition that we weren't expected to "learn the law" but "think like lawyers." But while I wasn't getting an education on legal procedure, I was learning everything about the upper-crust. My classmates weren't like the kids from Vegas or even the poker players. They were cultured. They ate fast food ironically. They talked about where they traveled (which I learned was a key distinction between the haves and have-nots). My girlfriend grew up with an au pair. I tried not to judge them.

I was deep in Obama territory and every well-to-do Chicagoan at the party (there were many) had a story linking them to Barack and Michelle. The party host pulled out a picture with Joe Biden and used the phrase "Uncle Joe," except he really considered Biden an "Uncle Joe" and I wouldn't realize that phrase was something for everyone else until a few years.

I tried to float along with my own story about betting on the election. It was exciting to me. But each time I told someone, I was regarded with a mix of worry and intrigue.

Like a pet raccoon. This wasn't Las Vegas. It was the first time I learned gambling wasn't normal.

Making matters at the party worse, I was severely underdressed. A t-shirt and jeans to watch TV made sense to me. But the Illinois natives were dressed up to see their darling Senator-turned-President secure another term in the White House. I sensed they thought I was exploiting the American virtue of the Electoral College. Maybe I was drunk. Regardless, I didn't need their judgment. Or their broadcast. I checked the numbers from the betting site, InTrade, on my phone. Something I'd been doing so often, I had made the gambling site my homepage.

InTrade was an online betting house that let you wager on almost any indeterminate event around the world from the comfort of your home. Oscar races, election results, even the next Game of Thrones character to die. There were markets for every possible race—House, Senate, state elections, ballot initiatives. It was like a racetrack for Washington D.C.

The site worked as follows:

If Obama was listed as 40% to win, every $40 bet collected $100 ($60 from the losing side). This was the same for every election, race, or prop. Free market at its finest. The fact that Obama was an underdog seeking re-election meant there were delusional McCain supporters who were richer than they were smart.

As I understood it, Obama was a lock to win. I wasn't just influenced by the Young Democrats around me. A friend I met through the poker forums—Ben—introduced me to FiveThirtyEight.com. FiveThirtyEight was started by a statistician, Nate Silver, as a blog. It quickly grew to be one of the top election prediction sites after 2012. I didn't know much about Silver, but I knew Ben was a very good poker player and I fully trusted his resources. When I told our group chat about InTrade, he privately messaged me

Seat Open

and said we should push it to the limit; so not knowing any better, we did.

Our wounds were still fresh from a year and a half earlier when the Department of Justice shut down the three biggest poker sites. All of the group had lost money. It was the extinction of a workforce. Several we knew were "poker refugees," forced to move to Mexico or Canada to continue playing their online game. The DOJ hadn't said a word about returning funds. We needed a win.

I loaded the money I had for law school into the account. I waited for some guardian angel to appear on my shoulder and stop me, but that never happened. Why would it? This was a great bet. My justification was an Obama reelection was the surest thing I would see for a while. I trusted Ben as a gambler—especially considering he had his own skin in the game.

Ben sent me five figures— most of his bankroll— to bet on Obama. Ben was graduating college in Chicago and would be playing poker full-time. He wanted to pad his entry into the profession and doubling his roll would do that. Ben had taken a good, middle class upbringing and leveraged it into success as a poker player. He represented the bookish, well-mannered new wave of grinder, emboldened by success online. As kind as he was intimidating. I respected Ben because he saw the well-tread path of 9-to-5 success and completely rejected it. He was one of the only people who I gave a street pass to for not coming from a broken home.

I put almost all of our bets on Obama between 40% and 50% to win the election. We could more than double our money. Try as we might, there wasn't a universe where we could see Obama losing. But winning would only be half the battle.

Back at the party, InTrade listed Obama at 56%. I knew to not overreact to small swings, but this was the largest lead he'd held since Ben and I invested. I considered selling our position for the guaranteed ~12% gain, but that was foolish. Obama looked like he would actually win this.

My girlfriend and I left the party early. I could hear about returns in Wisconsin only so many times. We went back to her apartment where her roommates watched more election coverage. Fox News, not CNN. They stayed away from the party being staunch Republicans. They knew about my bet and while they disliked who I was betting on, they respected my entrepreneurial acumen (although handicapping the Electoral College still left a bad taste in their mouths).

I saw returns coming from state races Ben and I had bet, also based on Silver's models— Colorado and Florida, both traditional Republican states, going Democrat. In the more intimate setting, I didn't mind sweating the voting results as they came in. The four of us ate ice cream and my girlfriend and her roommates briefed cases for our Property class while I updated Ben. I wish I could say there was uncertainty in the race, but even on Fox, Obama led wire to wire. It seemed like the whole country had voted Democrat. Even the Florida and Colorado bets came in. Who had bet McCain? At his own election party, Ben was excited, but just barely. He looked at the election like any other +EV wager. Solely mathematical.

The polls had closed and Obama traded at 99%. Not wanting to jeopardize our winning bets, Ben and I made an executive decision. We took advantage of the perpetual market, the buying and selling of presidential likelihoods, and cashed out. There were several users willing to buy almost certain bets for 99c on the dollar and wait for them to clear through the site's slow bet scorers in exchange for the free 1-2%. No different than third party check cashers working next to the foreman's office. The internet was the future.

Sitting in bed with my girlfriend asleep next to me, chest and face lit blue by my laptop, I requested an immediate

Seat Open

withdrawal to my bank account. I looked into the dark room and thought it strange that I was doing something so important on a tiny screen and the world around me was silent. I thought it might make me feel powerful, but I felt very much the opposite.

Every day, every hour, multiple times an hour, I checked my transaction history for updates. The withdrawal read: *Requested*. There was a thrill one day later when the withdrawal status changed from "*Requested*" to "*Processing*". The wheels were turning. I updated Ben.

I tried to focus on classes, but I was a temporary law student and a permanent gambler. I wasn't able to concentrate past the stinging rashness of my decision. I had bet almost every dollar to my name. My closest friends who I had met from online poker bet most of what they had, too. I was borrowing money to eat Taco Bell. To make things worse, I was the puppeteer of the bet, keeping thousands of dollars of separate wagers organized in a Note file on my phone.

I lost sleep. InTrade was based out of Ireland, so they were six time zones ahead. This gave me an excuse to log in and check if progress was being made in the middle of the night. I pestered Customer Support with a nonexistent claim to see if I could get any timeline on my payout. Eventually, my withdrawal was listed as "*Awaiting Confirmation*" which I wasn't sure was progress but acted like it was.

Finally, one day, I checked the site in the back of my Contracts class, like I did dozens of times before, and sanction came from on high—"*Processed*."

Compared to checking InTrade, checking my bank account every fifteen minutes was a breeze. Two days later, the money was there. I had never seen my account brimming before. Albeit, most of the money belonged to Ben, checking my account balance gave me a rush. The same feeling from ordering an expensive dinner, winning a big poker hand, getting noticed behind the wheel of a nice car. Not just surviving but thriving. Nothing more than the ancient feeling of dopamine.

By the end of the week, I was on an Amtrak train to Chicago to see Ben.

"Home sweet Homewood!," the conductor bellowed as we passed from farmland through the roller-coasting Chicago suburbs—working class neighborhoods slowly getting better, then much, much worse, until we were in the bustling downtown heart of the city.

I had only been to Chicago a few times, but its most dominant elements, pulling into Union Station, were the city's history as the centerpiece of Midwest shipping and its ability to leverage its past becoming a hub of entertainment, hospitality, and culture. Chicago was very Midwest in its logic—life followed money.

Ben picked me up on Wacker Drive and we caught up. The trip was obviously celebratory, capped by Ben finishing his last batch of finals. While he didn't doubt the pro poker dream, Ben knew it was in his best interest as a poker player and as a son to finish his degree. It might've seemed like a waste, but other players dumped their winnings into the sports book, so who could really judge. His major was something in business.

We were eager to go to the bank to collect our winnings, but the branches were already closed. We went back to Ben's apartment which he shared with a roommate who was equally apathetic to his studies but without any gambling talent, so I mostly ignored him.

I had heard about Chicago's nightlife and I wanted to see it for myself, so we resolved to go to the bars. We dressed up for a night on the town. I spent my entire life in Las Vegas and wasn't used to actual weather, much less this corn-fed Illinois version of November. I kept a jacket

Seat Open

on to prepare for the biting cold and understood this was just how people out here lived. Coat check made sense.

We went to a local bar that was painfully similar to the ones in the college town back at law school. We drank cups of sticky blue liquor with other Chicago collegiates. Ben's roommate jumped up and down to rap music, with everyone else there, his gold chain flopping on his bed of chest hair.

We went to another bar that better fit my expectation for Chicago nightlife. Bottles of champagne, women dancing on couches, rumors the Chicago Bulls were in the building.

We drank $15 drinks, cautious in our celebrating, allowing ourselves the paranoia of success, fearing that our money would be confiscated from my bank account in some roundabout way. Walking home, I saw rats scurrying in the shadows through an alley. Chicago seemed like a cleaner version of New York, or at least a colder, more habitable one. We got back to the apartment and I passed out on the couch, bundled in a blanket.

The city froze and thawed every morning.

The next day, we drove to the bank. Ben and I wouldn't feel safe until the funds were in our hands. I had a lie planned for the teller about putting a down payment on a property, in case they questioned me. In the gambling world, stories of money being held by your bank, sent back, or flagged were all too common. It wasn't your money, they just let you use it.

I walked into a Bank of America in Chicago's financial district, ready to defend my withdrawal. But I had clearly overthought the whole thing. I was snake bitten by the DOJ. The teller I approached, incredibly bubbly, didn't have a problem putting what I considered a large amount of cash into a paper envelope. I showed her my driver's license and she slid it right back over. Minutes before, I

Blockhead

had been asking Ben if we needed to call ahead. It only served to remind me no matter how much of a shark you think you are, you're always a guppy in another pond.

    I went to where Ben was parked, waiting anxiously, and gave him the envelope. He tossed it into his glovebox, and like that, secured the next rung. Ben drove back to his apartment and we decided to celebrate by getting shitfaced at a casino. Ben's usual haunt was the Horseshoe, forty-five minutes away in Gary, Indiana. There was an Illinois law that forced the casino to be built in the small town just outside city limits, severely depressing the surrounding economy and everyone who went there. I had a deep respect for all pros who maintained a semblance of life by not living in Las Vegas.

    We got high and made our way to a nearby Five Guys to fill up on greasy food before drinking. It was packed with teenagers, the kind I used to count myself amongst on the back of the bus. They stole soda with water cups and planned pointless all-nighters while Ben and I stood out, eating cheese fries in shirts and slacks. I was desperate to be them again. Another street kid. I realized I was high, thinking too much, and kept eating.

    We went to meet a shuttle for the casino in front of a closed shopping center next to Five Guys. Standing on the darkened sidewalk, I wasn't sure if maybe we had messed up the schedule, when a black shuttlebus turned the corner. We climbed on and saw that everyone else, including the driver, was Asian between the ages of fifty and sixty-five. Ben explained to me that this was a major pastime for older Asian degens. I wasn't surprised considering my dad's favorite casino had a similar crowd being near Chinatown. Gambling served as a community hub, as bizarre as that was.

    The shuttle took us through Chicago, trekking north. We made a few more stops, slowly adding passengers, until by

Seat Open

some weird work of the Devil, we were exactly full and continued onto the interstate.

We pulled off somewhere near a busy rest-stop Burger King and a string of overpriced gas stations. We were here. A tall building remarkable for being a casino only if you've seen hundreds like it before. We were dropped inside, and Ben had the foresight to look up timetables for departing buses. They ran less frequently, not surprising.

I noticed most of the olds lining up and receiving a payout of $20 from a mystery man. I wasn't sure if this was some kind of sketchy affiliate business, paying them just to show up, but I didn't want to press it further.

Ben and I found the poker room, but took a pit stop at the bar outside. We ordered doubles and paid too much attention to the basketball game. We ordered two more. Then two more. Only then was it time to play low stakes poker.

We were seated at a $1/$2 game and ordered more drinks, getting blind drunk. While I eased into the behaviors of the carefree gambler, Ben couldn't help but dominate. Ben played like the high stakes regular he was, shoving his stack in with reckless abandon, running over the table. The smarter regulars scurried off. Ben made another thousand in profit, and I managed to pocket a few hundred in the fray. After a couple of hours, we tipped too much and cashed out.

Ben and I stumbled to the departing shuttle lobby. It had the forsaken presence of a bus depot down to the reflective tile and impoverished vending machines. Ben and I bought an armful of Gatorades. I sank into a bench and the other people moved around me like grey phantoms, hovering through the air. This unpleasant feeling mixed with the Orange electrolytes and whiskey already inside me, and I felt a familiar nausea.

I thought about finding a bathroom but before I could, the bus pulled up. I knew in my heart if we missed this bus, we might never leave the Horseshoe. It was time for the hour and a half ride home.

I put my head against the window as Ben, also drunk, was fortunately lucid enough to track the stops and point us home. In the queasy blackness that came when I closed my eyes, I tried to balance on to the success of our scheme— not of the money—but of leaving the Reservation and coming back with a pelt. This thought kept me conscious, upright.

In the dark, I heard Ben. I felt the bus pull to a stop. "Let's go."

I scooted away from the window and silently puked on my seat.

I wiped my mouth and got to my feet, blurrily following Ben off. I felt bad, but only a bit. I had gotten seasick on Charon's ferry. Appropriately, when we stepped off the bus, I was hit with loud sounds, angry voices, and a burning, yellow light.

I thought we were in Hell. We were at a "Rock and Roll McDonald's."

Ben told me we had gotten off one stop early, although I'm not sure if the decision was a conscious one. But now that we were here, we went inside and ordered. Chicken nuggets, for some reason, seemed like the safest bet and, on a streak, was another gamble I won.

Ben and I made it back to his apartment, and I crashed on the couch until 8 AM when it was time to leave for my train. I woke up freezing again and bundled with every spare blanket and pillow in Ben's apartment. The Midwest cold didn't make any sense. Why did people live here?

I checked the morning news, which meant scrolling through Twitter, and saw something that froze me colder— InTrade had been shut down by the CFTC. According to the statement, the site offered "unregulated derivatives trading" and was now, well, being regulated. How a

Seat Open

Europe-based website could be affected by the actions of the United States Commodities overseer was another question entirely. Evidently, we just missed Gamble Gamble's bad luck by a matter of days. I told Ben about the confiscation.

"Holy shit," he muttered.

We processed facts as they became available. There were posts on sports betting message boards—and on our own poker forums—about users having money stuck on InTrade. No withdrawals were being processed and no one knew when they would be. This was painfully reminiscent of Black Friday. We had seen this all before.

Ben congratulated me and thanked me at the same time. If we had waited instead of selling early for a little less, we could've lost everything. For once, things had worked out well. I almost felt guilty, which must've been the feeling of success. We ate breakfast at a place near the train station and Ben dropped me off. I boarded my Amtrak back to law school and sank into my seat, hungover.

As the train filled up, I took inventory of the past week. I hadn't read for class which, fortunately in law school, didn't matter. The CFTC statement and accompanying case law were instructive enough. I closed my eyes for a nap, wondering if I'd ever fully shirk my gambling habits or if they weren't habits but conscious, furtive pursuits. Then, I remembered a chore I had been putting off the entire time Ben and I had been betting on the election.

I had forgotten to vote.

Blockhead

Buffalo Nick and the Champagne Room

The summer before law school, I moved onto the Strip to be as close to the action as possible. The Meridian Condominiums were populated almost entirely by poker players and strippers. It was natural. If strippers were lions, poker players were the hyenas. The watering hole dwindled every day.

The Meridian was a sprawling complex with three pools, one armed with cabanas and grills, and one for adults only. The apartment was a two-bedroom that came furnished but was so manicured it was difficult to feel comfortable. The world's most famous cities were inexplicably painted on a living room wall. My bedroom had a large bed, pillowy soft, in a room with giant blackout curtains. I could come home from gambling at 8AM and sleep like a baby. The Meridian knew its audience.

I found a roommate on a poker message board—Cory Adams. Other than my street kid upbringing—five of us sleeping in the "mattress room" on rotation— I never had a roommate. But I wanted to enrich my social experience, and I was told poker houses were worth the anxiety. Cory was tall and thin with a Kennedy-type charm that kept him from being goofy. He had a frattiness that was frowned upon in 2019 but was still fine in 2011. I knew him from our group chat as a successful tournament pro.

I bought ten percent of Cory's tournament buy-ins. He was playing a slew of tournaments and I didn't plan on playing any, seeing that specific grind as too anguishing. Investing in Cory was a way to increase my tournament exposure through a better player without having to be one myself.

The day we moved into our unit, as we passed our neighbors, we were hit with the overpowering stench of

Seat Open

marijuana. I found out many of the complex's residents were midlevel drug dealers, always flush with cash, wanting locations near the casinos. Completely understandable. As close to the action as possible.

In late May, when players were still trickling in, I flew Allison out. Allison was a long distance flirtation and the hyper-religious best friend of my friend, Sarah. We met when they both attended art school, and we stayed in touch when they graduated. I visited her when I was in the Midwest. She wanted to come to Vegas, but didn't have the discretionary money. What good were these poker chips for?

Our upbringings—hers god-fearing, mine godless—rarely came between our romance. We both saw the world for what it was and tried to make the best of it. She went to church; I went to the casino. If God had a problem with the arrangement, he couldn't be reached.

When she got in, we spent our days trying different restaurants around the Strip, and I showed her the sights. We spent one night making cupcakes. Things went well. Until I took Allison to Musashi.

Musashi was a tepanyaki grill run by a man named Tiger. If you were a poker player in Las Vegas, you had eaten there. Musashi was known for its crowded walls of photographs. The walls were covered with framed pictures of Tiger and any famous person who had eaten there. Kobe Bryant, Sandra Bullock—even local celebrities like Carrot Top and Lance Burton. Musashi also served as the unofficial poker equivalent of Cooperstown, the baseball Hall of Fame.

What made the walls so crowded were the dozens of pictures of Tiger and various poker players. Not just WSOP winners, but successful cash game players, even groups of accomplished online pros. There were several photos with Tiger and guys I considered friends. I was jealous. Having

Blockhead

my photo up at Musashi wall was the accomplishment I always had in the back of my mind.

I loved Musashi even without the pictures. The food was delicious. The other chefs, plucked from Food Network or the best ranks of Benihana, consistently provided one of the best restaurant experiences in all of Las Vegas. They carted their tepanyaki accoutrement from grill to grill and half-performed/half-cooked in seatings that lasted between one and four hours. Tiger was partial to longer performances.

Musashi was also known for its "Happy Hour." After midnight, their prices dropped significantly and more risqué festivities took place. Penis-shaped beer bongs, mini flamethrowers, and once, when the chefs were sufficiently drunk, they let my friend cook behind the grill.

The last time Cory and I went to Musashi, Tiger had worn an apron with a built-in dildo and told us we'd be added to the wall the next time we came in. I was ecstatic. I figured this was the perfect place to bring Allison on one of her last nights in town. She had heard me mention Musashi before and said she wanted to experience the poker side of the city. I told her we might get our pictures taken, the blissful idiot I was.

We walked into the restaurant and were seated immediately. We passed framed poker players on the way to our grill, me pointing them out to her. We were sat with three other couples, plunged into anxiety-by-osmosis. Not normally nervous, the intimacy of four dates meant the tepanyaki grill was floating on expectations. I was seasick. Tiger approached our table and announced he would be our chef. I felt things settle around me. I was glad he was our captain. But neither of us knew there would be no photographs, no lifeboats, no survivors.

While Tiger was setting up, he greeted me and introduced himself to Allison, which I thought was a kind gesture. He told her specifically, he hoped she enjoyed the

Seat Open

show. He turned on the gas, lit the flame, and immediately dove into the crudest, most sexually explicit display of food I'd seen outside of hardcore pornography.

The spatulas clanged against the metal grill, and with amazing dexterity, Tiger made a girthy rice-penis that doubled as both side dish and foreplay. I looked at Allison to see what she thought— she wasn't smiling.

In fact, she looked pissed. Fuck. The pre-dread apprehension hit, I felt from on-high that this would not be a good night. This had not been a good idea.

Tiger slid the spatula under the rice-cock and softly tapped it, giving the illusion of throbbing. He sprinkled seasoning on the penis saying, "Oh God, I love that. Give it to me, baby."

I turned back to Allison to see if her opinion had changed. Her lips were pursed. I considered pointing out the irony, questioning the foundation of her outrage, but even I wasn't that naive. Discussing the night was eons away. For now, we had to live through it.

The other couples were having a good time and I tried to sit on the fence between interested and apathetic while praying a fire would break out. Tiger took out a miniature Barack Obama figurine holding a barrel around his body. He pressed a button and the barrel flipped up revealing a spring-loaded cock. To make matters worse, I remembered Allison was related to a key Republican Party leader. The night was lost.

But for Tiger, it was very much still starting. "I'm going to go around and try to get a read on your favorite sex positions."

I saw Allison clench her fists under the table. Would it be better if Tiger guessed right? Worse?

Tiger pointed to the first couple. "Doggy," he said to much laughter. So much for that.

"Cowgirl," more laughs. He kept going.

He pointed to Allison. "Feet on shoulders."

Blockhead

"Whatever."

Tiger moved on and it was Allison's turn to look at me, to be sure I heard the flatness in her answer loud-and-clear. I had made the mistake of opening the door to our bedroom and nothing would be left but fire and brimstone.

Tiger cooked entrees, a mix of beef and chicken. And shrimp. Allison had abandoned feeling anything other than clear and obvious contempt, and she stared at the grilling shrimp like they were all sizzling in Hell together. As Tiger grilled, taking his time with specialized sauces, I realized he was telling a story, of course, about how horny the shrimp were. And as he told the story, of course, he made the shrimp fuck each other.

The shrimp were paired off and engaged in a multitude of sex acts, as Tiger described them. Anal, threesomes, gangbangs. His knife moved with surgical precision forcing the shrimp into position after position like a manic porn director.

As the shrimp were almost fully cooked, Tiger went to sauce them. He grabbed a giant cylinder of a spicy soy mix and, in a grand climax, sprayed it over the grill, mimicking a massive shrimp orgasm, accompanied with grunts and moans. The whole thing was quite majestic, mortifying Allison aside.

Tiger served the entrees, breathless. I was shocked. It was a great demonstration of ability. The best Musashi performance I'd ever seen. But Allison was shaking in rage. Not shaking—vibrating. I prayed she went supernova and took us all out.

"I'm not eating that," she managed to say.

I considered where to align myself. Did Tiger do something wrong? Did I have no manners? Did our tablemates? Did it matter? Talking about lewd sex acts at dinner seemed totally normal. The only time I prayed to God that entire summer was then and there, and I asked for a gas leak. No pain.

Seat Open

"Was something wrong?" Tiger asked, legitimately concerned for Allison's meal. He had no idea.

"That's... just... not how we do things where I'm from," was Allison's surprisingly deft complaint.

Tiger gave a sideways explanation—apologizing she didn't like the show—and left for another table shortly thereafter. No pictures were to be taken. Allison picked at her food, not eating any shrimp, and we left.

The entire dinner took about three hours and the desert temperature had cooled significantly. Nonetheless, when we got back to the apartment, Allison was still steaming. I was lectured about how unchivalrous it was to let Tiger cook like that and how insulting the entire experience had been. She mentioned bringing the experience up to a church group I had previously never heard about. She was offended in a way I didn't think people actually got offended, outside of movies.

We didn't have sex again until the next day.

Before Allison left, she gave me a small ceramic pig made from South American volcanic rock that was allegedly infused with good luck. She got it from a tourist shop that specialized in such things. It felt brittle. I thanked her. I'd take all the help I could get. After she left, I puked for three days. I wasn't sure if it was stress from being performative or food poisoning (divine punishment), but I didn't leave the apartment for a week.

One day, Cory suggested gambling on the Strip together. Feeling better, I agreed, and we went to the Bellagio. Cory moved with immediacy and I followed him to the roulette wheel. He revealed he had an expert strategy: only bet on prime numbers. He rattled off some properties of prime numbers that, if he had started rooted in facts, quickly delved into spirituality, if not mysticism.

Apparently, I was betting against a massive edge and invoking the wickedness of the universe, and definitely being a big fucking dumbass if I didn't bet every prime number— 1, 2, 3, 5, 7, 9, 11, 13, 15, 17, 19, 23, 27, 29, 31; and yes, I had obviously forgotten 2 was a prime number.

I knew it was nonsense, but gambling is entertainment and it felt good to have more of a strategy than betting on the birthdays of ex-girlfriends. We started in on the strategy and it struck like wildfire. Despite the fact that the betting style is really just a complicated way of betting a third of the board, we were winning ninety percent of the spins, pocketing black $100 chips of profit.

A group of college kids, our age, came to the table and were silently impressed with how quickly we were able to fill the board, prime numbers becoming muscle memory. They regarded us as pros. Cory and I had ascended as summer degenerates.

As the WSOP picked up and everyone arrived in Vegas, we met up with others from our group chat.

Most were tournament pros and all similar to the point of near-parody. Like most poker players, they dressed almost exclusively in hoodies and basketball shorts. They were inseparable from their backpacks. Ate like children. Smoked like rappers. I saw it as a way to cope with the mental peaks and valleys, sometimes enduring dozens of tournaments without winning anything, down tens of thousands of dollars in buy-ins to their investors. It wasn't uncommon for a tournament pro to win $800,000 in a tournament and still be stuck in the hole for the year.

Making up the group was:

Marine Roy – part of the "work hard / play hard" **contingent.** Marine Roy was a short, recently divorced ex-Marine. He was probably the worst poker player of the group and complained the most, an awful combination. He was built like a brick shithouse and about as crude.

Nick – an accomplished, quiet Midwest tournament pro. The glue of the group.

Seat Open

L.T.—frequently confused for brothers with Nick, his father was also a successful player (known in the community as "Big L.T.")

Buffalo Nick – appropriately named, hailing from Buffalo. Buffalo Nick was a med student who moonlighted as a tournament player. He was known for always carrying $25k in his pocket.

When I asked about the $25k, Buffalo Nick gave me his prepared answer. "In case I find a good game."
"So you carry that cash with you always?"
"Yes."
"In case there's a really juicy high stakes poker game."
"Exactly."
Nick chimed in, "He was ready when we were in the sporting goods aisle at Wal-Mart last night."
Everyone laughed. Buffalo Nick's neurosis clearly stemmed from a missed opportunity in his past. Otherwise, he was one of the more put together degenerates. As a med student, he mostly contained his playing to the summer, but he was always looking for another game, playing a full schedule of tournaments.

Together, we mostly played cards at their house, gambled on the Strip, ate sushi, or drove in-between. A WSOP house is like a temporary frat house with much lazier, smarter degenerates. Unsurprisingly, some players had backgrounds in Greek Life at Big Ten schools. There was always some combination of booze and soda, no food except for leftovers and hot chips, and no toilet paper (but many paper towels). Weeks went by in a blur.

Cory and I were frequent visitors of the Rio.
Each summer, the Rio was every poker player's combination workplace-and-church. To enter meant crossing the endless pavement of the parking lot. Cars lined up row after row, each driven by a competitor trying to win

fortunes on a table somewhere. Triple digit temperatures were the norm. It was common to see a hoodied, black figure shuffling, stuck between the heat beating down and radiating up. No matter if someone played high stakes or low, famous or unknown, the heat made everyone wither.

Once past the parking lot, you were greeted by the smokers' circle. Players on break took relief with a cigarette and misters spraying fresh water into the burning desert air, above signs advertising water conservation. Bolder players slyly smoked weed, unwilling to make the trek back to their cars. "Peeling bananas" was the code word.

Walking through the doors, you were hit with a blast of arctic air. It felt like a relative ice hotel, and inside everyone was bundled up for a constant 63 degrees. Sweatshirts, beanies, jogging pants. The hoodies every poker player wore gave protection from the elements inside and out. You forgot about the burn of one extreme as soon as you were in the other.

Next to the entrance was the treacherous poker kitchen with its $4 bananas and $17 chicken teriyaki bowls. Reports of food poisoning or alien items in the food would appear a few times a year and be knowingly ignored. Poker players guessed and hoped, desperate for any meal less than a half mile walk from the rest of the casino. The poker kitchen was just another place to gamble.

Moving from the kitchen, the hallways were lined with rows of booths hoping to sell wares to impulsive gamblers. Poker books, signature sunglasses, WSOP merchandise, and phone chargers. The phone charger vendors were a special class of creature. They sold 400% marked up phone accessories notable for breaking within days. Only the most desperate of poker player, with no other way to charge their mobile, would go to them. Their sales tactics were similar to carnival barkers, slinging whatever crude remark they could, hoping to convert any attention into a sale or just wanting to spurn annoyance. They were universally hated by a group of people who bet against each other for a living.

Inside the Rio's convention center was the WSOP's heart of felt—the special camera-circled table where the final hands of the biggest tournaments were played. With rows of bleachers for spectators, this was where everyone—player and fan alike—wanted to end up. With its unsightly steel architecture supporting blinding lights and signage, the final table was affectionately termed the "Thunderdome" by those forced aboard.

I entered the Thunderdome to cheer for a few friends, but despite near misses, there were no bracelets that summer. One afternoon, after losing the daily $250 tournament, I was making my way to the hellish parking lot when I ran into Nick. He told me everyone from their house was going out to the Strip, celebrating a friend in town, and invited me along.

Nick and I met with the group—including Buffalo Nick and Marine Roy—at a dueling piano bar. It wasn't long before we made friends with a group of women at another table—tourists from the South. I was more than happy to play wingman, but what I didn't know was that some of my co-pilots were on a kamikaze flight.

Buffalo Nick and Marine Roy were hitting on the same woman. They were all very drunk, and she was playing them both exactly evenly; God bless her. At one point, I took a picture from behind them of Buffalo Nick's arm around her and Roy holding her hand. It was unseemly. One way or another, she cut ties with both of them and we all ended up in Nick's friend's hotel room shitfaced. The groups wanted to reconvene as everyone was impossibly scattered, more or less a typical Vegas night.

But Marine Roy was livid.

He marched up and down the hotel room shouting not at Buffalo Nick, who was puking in the bathroom and likely the reason he was (we thought) going to bed alone, but he was berating Nick. He was yelling about being "left behind by his bros." It was mostly gibberish—likely the result of a summer (and largely a year) spent losing—and he was taking it out on Nick.

Nick tried to justify some trivial point and Marine Roy slapped him, open-handed, across the face. I was so surprised, my mouth fell open. Even Buffalo Nick called out from just above the toilet bowl, "Did someone get slapped?" But Nick, clutching a red cheek, yelled at Roy and thankfully let it go; everyone's drunkenness making it all no big deal.

Roy calmed down, and as the night came to a close, he asked if he could crash on Cory and I's couch. I knew Cory was already asleep and much laxer than me, so I agreed and we went to the taxi stand.

On the way back to the apartment, Roy had a bigger ask—could he "call a girl?"

Before I could respond, he flew into a well-oiled story about being at rock bottom and how everything would be momentarily better if only he could call over an escort to our couch. I told him to fuck off, but he kept pleading. He brought up his divorce. Did I know he had a kid? It wasn't easy making child support payments as a tournament pro. Roy made a point to say how he'd used "this site" (Backdoor) plenty of times before, and I had nothing to worry about. He made it seem like he was a VIP exclusive member and the woman would be chauffeured by winged horses.

As Roy looked up the number, I did my own Googling. I didn't find many reviews, but instead hooker horror stories. I was filled with visions of masked men kicking in the door and robbing us blind. This was a cliché in our industry, wasn't it? Could Marine Roy be setting us up? But he wasn't a very good poker player, and I probably could've seen that coming a mile away. More than likely, he was a

Seat Open

lonely guy just wanting to get laid. I relented, swayed by some argument about the free market or human urges and said he could "call a girl."

We got to the apartment and I showed him the couch, grabbed the biggest, sharpest knife from the kitchen, and went to my bedroom. I slid a dresser in front of my door and put the knife on the end table closest to me. I took all my high denomination poker chips and hid them throughout my bedroom in various stashes. On the off-chance Marine Roy was going to get rolled by the escort, I was prepared to lose the minimum. I fell asleep wondering when she'd get there, if I'd hear them, and why I had agreed in the first place.

The next morning, I stayed in my bedroom until 9 AM when I heard noise outside that told me Cory was awake. I checked on Roy who was asleep in a mess of sheets and updated Cory on last night's visitor. Roy woke up and let us know his night was very successful in spite of the fact the 5'4" woman he called for had a "tire blowout" and was replaced by someone 6'1".

"I like them tall, though."

Roy thanked us again and took a cab home. I didn't use the couch for the rest of the summer.

A week later, Cory came into the apartment at 1AM, exhausted and overjoyed. He had made the final nine of a tournament at the Venetian and was the massive chip leader. They would play the final table tomorrow. First prize was $150k, which meant $15k for me if Cory won. I had never had a five-figure score. It would be glorious. Whatever my plan was previously, I was now going with Cory tomorrow, playing the role of supportive housemate, sweating my investment.

I woke up at 7AM the next day. Cory and I parked in the Venetian's underground parking garage. I noted we were on LEVEL B by way of an upside-down sign.

Blockhead

A poker game, especially a tournament, is one of the least spectator-friendly events imaginable. "Sweating Cory" meant sitting around the tournament area with our friends, triangulating chip updates between a TV monitoring progress and glances at Cory's table—twenty feet away behind velvet ropes. What made it so engaging was the thousands of dollars to personally gain from the results. The entire experience was some sort of gambling torture device, like betting on backwards horseracing.

Cory was easily the most experienced player at the table and had a mountain of chips in front of him. I was too focused on the money to realize these positive indicators almost certainly foreshadowed his defeat.

Cory bluffed off a large amount of chips to a woman with bright pink hair who had a motorcycle boyfriend/dad cheering her on from the rail. Cory fell to 2nd in chip but was still the best player there. However, a few hands later, his success story took a turn.

Cory stood up from his seat, which signaled he was all-in for his tournament life. He had pocket tens against an Ace and a King of the chip leader. A coin flip.

Cory yelled out, "Damnit!"

It meant he had lost.

He hustled out of the isolated tournament area and came to our group on the rail. He had finished eighth for $4,000. Expecting to be there for the entire day, we were done before lunchtime. We congratulated and consoled Cory on his success and early bust. Instead of the five-figure payday I had already mentally spent, I would be getting $400.

I escorted Cory to the Cashier for his payout. There was an unwritten gambling rule that I was allowed to feel bad, but certainly no worse than Cory. Somehow, we had found a way to feel bad about winning money. We went back to the parking garage. Level B, where I parked my car. But it wasn't there.

Seat Open

I looked around. It had been an exhausting day, but I was fairly certain—and Cory was too—that my car should be where it wasn't. We noted the upside-down sign. The garage was only so large. My car was nowhere in sight, and I was pressing the alarm on my car remote as superstition at this point. Something was wrong.

We searched the entire floor, but my car wasn't there. Outside, the 114-degree July sun cooked the underground garage; we were wandering around in a 90 degree oven. This was inadvisable, even for a Vegas native like me.

We went back to the casino floor and found Security. I explained the situation. I drove an older Honda Civic not worth much except for when you needed to go somewhere, if that mattered. It was clear Security thought we were drunk tourists parked on the wrong floor, and we waited downstairs while a security guard on bicycle checked every floor of the parking garage for my car.

I saw the frustration on Cory. He had just lost a tournament and likely six figures in his mind. But he was a good guy and mostly buried it, knowing that I didn't intend to lose my car, per se. There was nothing that could be done other than what we were doing. Then, I thought about the spare key I kept in the glove box for no real reason and the fact that I may have left the car unlocked, an unfortunate habit to save ten precious seconds. Pride cometh, I suppose.

The Security Guard came back and, finding nothing, suggested checking the security cameras. Cory and I went back to the casino floor and waited for him to return when, yes, they saw my car drive away on tape a few hours ago. Case unfortunately closed. We took a taxi home and I called the police to file a report. The thought flashed that at possibly the exact moment Cory lost his tournament, I had lost my car. The opposite of serendipity. But like any decent card player, I tried to think through the logic of the stinging loss. Metro said they would dispatch someone in the morning and as soon as I hung up, the stolen car vanished from my mind.

Cory was intent on celebrating his win, now believing it necessary to ward off the bad juju that had overtaken our apartment. The two hours to get showered and dressed went on and on and on. I swung between wanting to improve on Cory's tournament "win" and my vehicular loss by going out, or staying-in, but getting shitfaced regardless.

At 9PM, we headed to the Bellagio. It was still early in the night, so we decided to gamble first. What could we lose? Cory was eager to start at the roulette wheel but when we got there, I found a total absence of mood. Even our prime numbers couldn't save us. All of our bets were completely mechanical. Winning or losing didn't matter. Between the swings of money and cars, it was hard to feel anything about a spinning, white ball. I wondered what my high school friends were doing. I hadn't talked to them in years.

Cory and I continued to the club. Even though it was obvious to both of us neither wanted to be there, we knew we had to go. We met up with the same group of friends—L.T., Buffalo Nick, and Marine Roy, now silent about his escort. They were halfway through recollecting a funny story that happened at the Rio. Something about a famous tournament pro being publicly embarrassed. I was unable to pay attention.

Cory and I went to the bar where he told me he had my drinks covered. I didn't argue. Now loaded up with liquor, we integrated into the dancefloor. Cory gravitated to a mass of Asian co-eds, and I opted to dance alone, momentarily losing myself in the music, courting bliss, no matter how saccharine.

But after three song changes, I still couldn't shake the feeling of a 'we-go-to-different-schools' separation. I was with the crowd, but not in it. Everyone else was immersed in false apprehensions: worries of not having a good time,

Seat Open

not getting laid, not being drunk enough. I was pretending to be the same. Unsure as to what the day could hold. But I already knew it was terrible. I should've been at a dive bar instead. Frankly, it was impossible to have fun thinking so much.

I headed to the bathroom and ran into Cory, exiting. He clapped me on the shoulder.

"I just gave that guy the biggest tip he's ever gotten."

It was too loud to tell if he was joking or not.

"I asked the guy handing out towels what was the biggest tip he had had. He said $100. So, I gave him $100."

My first thought was that Cory had only *matched* this guy's biggest tip, but I knew that wasn't what he wanted to hear. If this was what he needed to do to reaffirm his position in the world, so be it. The towel guy gets a $100 tip. Cory gets to brag and forget his loss. This was a win-win.

Cory and I left the club, finally willing to accept defeat. The short taxi ride back was somber. Cory volunteered the information of the carjacking and the taxi driver immediately dumped his pity on us. Cory only tipped him $20.

Back in the apartment, Cory went to bed pretending to be more exhausted than he was. I went to my bedroom and locked the door. I took off my shoes and fell onto my comforter, letting my club clothes feel cool against my body. I looked at the TV. Allison's ceramic pig was staring at me. Her good luck charm. I jumped off the bed with a clarity that surprised me and threw the pig toward the bathroom, watching it shatter into a dozen grey pieces.

My buzzing phone woke me up. I was hungover, but not badly. I answered the call, sight unseen. "Yeah?"

"Las Vegas Metro Police Department. We're at the Meridian Apartments regarding a stolen vehicle."

Blockhead

I jumped out of bed, remembering everything. I found a shirt and shorts and jammed my feet into sandals with my dress socks still on.

I stumbled out of the apartment and realized I had no idea where the cops were. I took the stairs down into the parking garage, naively thinking they'd be where the car was supposed to be.

Instead, I found a mid-thirties man wearing a straw fedora, swim trunks, and an open Hawaiian shirt. He was pressed against a cement column in the garage, peeking at a police car parked outside of the parking structure. Our drug dealer neighbor had spotted my police officers.

"Don't worry, they're here for me," I said to him. He saw me and nodded, relaxing.

I went to the two police officers, hanging out by their car, and explained what happened. They were incredibly unstirred. This kind of thing happened to everyone, etc. I gave them as many details as I could, and nothing seemed special to them nor me. As I was giving my contact info I saw beyond them the drug dealer, tip-toeing back to our building like Wile E. Coyote toward another waiting trap. The Meridian had become a Saturday morning cartoon.

Cory and I survived on a diet of taxis, still years before rideshare was allowed to operate in Las Vegas. Spending more time stuck at the apartment, I was able to give a clear appraisal of how we were living—not well. At some point, Cory had split his bed frame and slept dangling off his uneven mattress. I still hadn't touched the prostitute-stained couch.

The trash was full, poker chips—some real, some fake—lay scattered around the living room, and the sink was overflowing with dishes including the tin Allison and I used to make cupcakes, now topped with mold. The metaphor was not lost on me. We were in decay.

Seat Open

I focused on the fact we were only there another three weeks, and that I was living the dream of thousands of amateur poker players worldwide.

Five days after I filed my police report, I received another call. They had found my car. I got a ride to North Las Vegas, thirty minutes from the Strip. I met with an officer at the impound lot, signed some papers, and was given my keys. The greatly anticipated interaction was surprisingly brief.

My car pulled up. I got in to appraise the condition under the scrutiny of my cell phone camera light. My first sight was the emptied Swisher Sweets covering the entire floor.

In the backseat of my car was the wardrobe of a homeless junkie:
  - a World Series 1998 sweater
  - dozens of stained, white tees
  - knockoff Nike New Balances
  - even more Swishers

Worse, every surface felt sticky. An invisible, gluey, oppressive stickiness. I drove around the corner to be out of sight from the police station and pulled over. I flung the door open and dumped the clothes in the middle of the street. Burning with embarrassment, I dug out the tobacco from my car as best I could, scraping into the upholstery. Had anyone seen me, they would've thought I was insane.

My car had a feeling of desperation that I knew would be permanent. It would always feel dirty. I drove back to the Meridian and parked, not bothering to lock it.

Cory and I started the long process of cleaning everything and packing up. The washing machine broke. The last week of our lease, a friend of a friend won $250k in a tournament. We went to the Spearmint Rhino, Las Vegas' preeminent strip club, to celebrate.

Inside was dark and labyrinthine. Every room had multiple stages with mostly nude women circulating high priced offers of private dances.

I sat in a booth, knowing we'd be leaving soon and not interested in any attention. Poker players tend to evoke their perversions in private, at least that's been my experience. Despite the fact that they should've known better, some of our group clearly felt special when these beautiful, dangerous women talked to them. Two dancers approached me. I told them I was gay, but they didn't believe me, so I told them I was poor and they disappeared.

Buffalo Nick vanished too, and the general consensus was that we were hungry. We left the stragglers behind and went for fast food.

We piled into L.T.'s SUV and he drove us to Sonic. While we sat in the drive-thru line within sight of the Strip, L.T. said, out of the blue, "I had a guy hit on me today."

L.T. had come out of the closet a year before, and he was one of the very few gay poker players I knew.

"That's a good thing," Nick said.

"Yeah, but it was weird for me."

None of us knew what to say. Had we forced L.T. to come with us? Was he annoyed? Was it a waste of money? Poker players can read people very well but only things they know to watch for. We dropped the topic entirely. The five of us spent $150 on burgers and chili fries and we ate like death row inmates.

The next morning, Cory and I got a text from the group. Buffalo Nick had come home at 4 AM and went straight to his room. He slept three hours and left for a flight home at 8 AM. He had spent every dollar of his $25K bankroll in the Rhino's champagne room. After that summer, I wasn't surprised. In the desert, every animal drinks its fill.

Seat Open

Ineffective Assistance of Counsel

    Bill Withers was 6'4" with a wooden leg and a debilitating gambling addiction.
    Bill had managed himself into a cozy position as head of the legal aid clinic I joined during my second summer of law school. He taught no classes, and his routine consisted of attending every law school function, competition, or lunch meeting for the free food. I always saw Bill holding a plate of finger sandwiches or a slice of Little Caesar's pizza. This was not a man suckered by Starbucks.
    It was the summer after Mike Neel's suicide and I wanted to commit myself to something that mattered, which I mistakenly thought was the law. I split that summer between the clinic, barely attending an Evidence class, and playing online poker for whiskey money. Every other law student was having an equally instructive summer with lessons in binge drinking and how to Google statutes.
    The only other student in my clinic was Nathan, a 1st year, which coupled with his Midwest disposition made him almost invisible. I could never figure out Nathan's MO, other than telling everyone who would listen that he had a girlfriend in med school two hours away. When he showed you pictures, he wanted you to see she was way out of his league. I figured Nathan could serve as a smoke screen. I could pick up the easier duties in the clinic to be a team player and let him "learn" through harder, more complex tasks. Nathan was the type that if he found out he was being Tom Sawyer'd, he probably wouldn't care.
    Four days of the week, Nathan and I would meet in Bill's office. The tan carpet and wood paneling gave a cramped feel—like the rumpus room at a crazy uncle's house. Shelves were crowded with law books. There was little attention to décor, only choices that prioritized utility

Blockhead

and speed, and not in that order. Even the way Bill packed papers into his faded satchel gave a feeling of someone not interested in planting roots. Someone with one eye always on the door.

The first time Bill talked about gambling, he caught me by surprise. One afternoon, Bill told me and Nathan how his wife had forced him on a diet. In a rushed stammer he said, "It's easy to cheat the diet. Just don't look at the calories. It's like being in the casino and not looking at your balance on the ATM receipt."

A lifetime dealing with gambling addicts and this was all I needed to hear.

It was clear Bill's enthusiasm in law was waning, whether he cared or even knew. Early in the summer, he would take out a thick legal tome from his shelves and ask us to flip to a specific legal term. He said this was because the stakes were high, and it was important to know exact definitions. Bill knew exactly how to waste half an hour.

That summer, our only case for the clinic was representing a 67 year old man named Henry Allen. Henry Allen's case was probably better suited for a human rights court than a criminal one. Henry admittedly spent every one of his Social Security checks on malt liquor 40s and crack cocaine. Henry claimed that he was owed $1.5 million for 190 years of back pay from the U.S. Government. His claim would've made him over 200 years old. We were litigating above our heads.

Henry was being evicted from his apartment in a large public housing building. Laying it out for us, Bill said Henry's case rested on his eviction notice-- while he was living in Apartment 6B, the eviction notice had been for Apartment 60B. I waited for Bill to continue but he didn't.

"We're in the right, and I'm not afraid to take this to the State Supreme Court."

Seat Open

Despite what amounted to a typographical error, Bill was pursuing the case like it was the trial of the century. He was milking a mis-click for all it was worth. Was this indicative of our clinic or the legal field at large? I felt a pang of despair.

As Nathan and I dug into the facts, the feeling worsened. Even with monthly social security checks, Henry hadn't paid rent in over six months. His file came with a long list of abstract charges and complaints from the building's management company. Among them, Henry riding his bicycle down his 6th floor hallway in the middle of the night. There were sanitary issues, plumbing mishaps, and finally, a note that in the winter months, Henry had run up an exorbitant gas bill choosing to heat his apartment by opening his oven and turning the heat all the way up. I wasn't sure how I'd feel if we stopped the eviction only for Henry to burn down his entire building. The fallout would guarantee Bill busywork for decades.

Henry was indicative of a small class of townsfolk the clinic was supposed to help. While I wasn't expecting the third act of some legal thriller, one where I convince a jury of Henry's alleged peers (which there were none) of his lifetime of innocence; somehow, I thought we could be doing more for Henry.

We tried to visit Henry at his apartment, but he was never home. We went to his listed place of employment, the neighborhood Methodist church. There, we met Henry Allen riding a lawn mower cutting the church's lawn. He was quiet with a stooped walk and rheumy eyes. When we explained who we were and that we wanted to help, that was the first time we heard Henry's impossible story of hundreds of years of pain and injustice. There was no room in his history for judgment.

We met Henry's pastor; a hawkish woman named Ms. Roberts. She said several of the parishioners had taken a liking to Henry and were keen on raising money for him. She talked about how, because of Henry's diminished mental capacity, she was in the process of obtaining his Power of Attorney and would have his checks sent to the Church to manage his funds. I wasn't sure if that's what was best for Henry, but better the devil you know.

The second time Bill mentioned gambling was the first time he mentioned trouble in his marriage. Nathan was drifting to sleep one afternoon in Bill's office while we were studying 19th-century property law for Henry's case.
"Are you tired?" Bill prodded.
"Yeah, I guess."
"What do you have to be tired about?" Bill asked. His wooden knee was without a joint which meant for an uncommon gait and whenever he sat at his desk, like now, he would hoist his leg up and drop it on the desk like a weapon at-ease.
"Do you know what I did last night?" he asked.
Nathan shook his head. I sat up, curious.
"I went to visit my father at his nursing home. We talked a little and he could remember me a little bit. We watched the basketball game on TV until the home closed at 10 PM. I called my wife and told her I had to get gas which meant I should be home around 11. But instead, I drove an hour and a half to Lucky Mary's—that slot parlor by Danville—and I had a hell of a run."
Bill was sitting up in his chair by now like he was in the middle of a war story and had just seen the enemy. I didn't tell him I was sorry his dad was ill. I certainly didn't tell him I knew Lucky Mary's.
"I took four hundred dollars from the ATM. I started playing around midnight and after a few hours I was up over a thousand!"
Bill's storytelling hit a fever pitch. "Now, I know I should've left then but—but I wanted to push my luck. I

went up and down and I got back down to one-sixty before I went back up to a thousand again." Bill nodded for good measure.

"Then you left?" I asked, but I already knew.

"Well, no."

Bill's face went blank. I had seen that look before. He was going where every degenerate gambler went to protect themselves from the results of yesterday's race. "I lost everything and I went home. Got in at about six. My wife was asleep, so I came here."

"You must be tired," I said.

Bill gave a goofy grin and nodded without saying anything else. I think he was happy I was paying attention.

A few days later, Bill said he would be out of town for the trial. He and his wife were spending a week in Big Sur for a marriage counseling retreat. He said this plainly and I wasn't surprised. The cost of a gambling addiction was always more than table stakes.

While I initially felt relieved, I realized this made things worse. Nathan and I would still be in trial, but Bill was arranging for another attorney to submit the worthless motion on his behalf. We were now failing Henry by proxy.

During that summer, I took an Evidence class taught by a successful local trial attorney— big fish, little pond. Keeping the class tolerable was a friend I'd made— the only other student hungover the first day of orientation— Justin. Justin's house was closer to school than my apartment, and the town was so dead I moved some clothes and paid his roommate $200 to use his place for the summer. Living with Justin maximized our time ordering takeout and bullshitting about women, which is what we mostly did together.

I was trying to focus away from the World Series of Poker, which was going on back in Las Vegas while the Illinois legal system was busy failing Henry. I maintained

Blockhead

the pretense that I wanted a life in either the law or the Midwest, something more civilized than gambling in the desert.

Nonetheless, I experienced the WSOP vicariously through updates from Ben and my good friend, Mike Brady. It was through Mike that I had met Ben, and they were representative of the new, young online players. Poker was a video game to them, and they used money to keep score. I had bought portions of every tournament they were playing—dozens in total, from a $1,000 turbo to a $25,000 high roller Mike had entered. Their success was my (fractional) success.

Every day, I considered the crossroads I was at. Was it better to be a competent mid-stakes poker pro or a low-grade attorney with a gambling problem? What was the worth society put on 'toeing the line'? None of the poker players I knew had offices and none had reserved parking spots, if you didn't count North Valet. They also didn't have to wear suits, either.

To distract from the poker tournaments that I wasn't playing, or the client I wasn't helping, Justin and I spent a lot of time with Gary.

Gary was from Michigan, quick to point out on "the mitten" exactly where, and was the brilliant son of simple, blue-collar parents. Gary regaled us with depressing tales of his childhood. All sorts of ironic dysfunction—doing his parents' taxes in middle school, or helping his racist grandmother amend her will. Gary's background also provided a wide range of social anxieties, like alopecia and insomnia.

When I wasn't first-mating the clinic into an iceberg, afternoons with Justin and Gary were spent languishing at Joe's Brewery with a pitcher of beer and a Bulls game. Joe's was locally infamous for its concoction of equal parts cheap beer and orange mix. The drink was called a lunchbox and came in a giant pitcher. While we should've been learning rules of character testimony, we ordered lunchboxes two at a time and entertained ourselves discussing Gary's relationships.

Justin and I teased Gary over his crush on Ella. Ella was a year below us, but in the same Evidence class and on Law Review with Gary. Ella had a disposition somewhere between charming and airy that made me once compare her to Luna Lovegood from Harry Potter. She was also our weed connect in town. Her bubbly exterior served as the perfect cover for razor sharp wit and an uncompromising attitude. No one knew that the same woman bringing homemade cookies to class and setting the curve in Property was also rolling joints and screening calls from her gangbanger ex-boyfriend.

It either made perfect sense or none at all.

The four of us started hanging out together, being some of the only students—people even—in the town. We filled out the back row.

One day at the gym, we decided Gary would invite Ella to study and eat a home-cooked meal. Gary loved cooking, and Justin and I were glad to see him pivot from baking depression cookies to better utilizing his talents. We were surprised by his initiative. Gary's date was set for the day before my deposition with Henry. We teased him endlessly, running his anxiety amuck.

Gary was appropriately cautious with details, fearing we'd ruin the date. He cooked Ella steak filet, mashed potatoes, green beans, and a pie from scratch. He had also organized a playlist that would be started while he cooked and continued at a low volume through the night.

Gary was, without a doubt, trying too hard.

Justin and I kept our phones handy and texted Gary crude messages throughout his date. We were playing NBA2K when Ella texted me. She said she was leaving dinner and asked if we wanted to smoke. Justin and I shared a look of disappointment tinged with guilt. Any way

Blockhead

we told this later, it would always look bad that we got stoned with our friend's date after how much effort he put in. We told Ella to come over.

Twenty minutes later, Ella was smoking us out and telling us about the dinner. We were surprised and a little disheartened that she claimed she had no idea the dinner was a date. This prompted her to pack another bowl. I thought about my impending deposition and we smoked until we were all rip-roaring high.

The next day, I slept in. I didn't go downstairs until 2PM. In our group text, Ben said he was boarding his flight from nearby Chicago to Las Vegas. Three people had already gotten kicked off the plane before they took off. The WSOP was in full swing. I was jealous.

I was getting ready for the deposition and Justin was getting ready for the gym when his phone rang.

"Fuck," he said after taking the call.

"What?"

"Gary is on his way over."

That wouldn't be concerning except the entire house smelled like weed, and Ella was the only person we knew still in town who had any. Gary knew this, too.

I ran to the bathroom, and possibly still stoned, sprayed Febreeze in every part of the house. If smelling like weed wasn't bad enough, weed and Tropical Delight™ was sure to raise suspicions.

Gary's car pulled up and Gary entered the house. He walked in, sniffing. If there was any doubt, the puzzled look on his face said we were toast. Gary winced in disgust.

"It smells like weed and air freshener." God damn.

Justin, who had been frozen by anxiety since Gary's call, started squirming in his seat. I forgot; he was not a poker player. Gary's face changed from displeasure to suspicion. His eyes narrowed.

Seat Open

"Let me guess. After dinner last night, Ella came over here and got you guys high." He wasn't joking, but he thought he was.

Justin darted from his seat, abandoning any pretense of dialogue. "Going to the car, bro." He headed right out the door, providing no help. There was only one thing I could do.

I looked right at Gary, and voice dripping with sarcasm, said, "Yeah, man. That's exactly what happened." And I slipped by, hidden by the truth.

I drove with Nathan to the deposition. We hadn't gone over questions— it didn't matter—Bill had some master plan. He reiterated the importance, he'd be running the show, and expected us to take diligent notes. I wasn't sure what we were doing there, seeing as how Henry never paid his rent and everyone knew he never paid his rent.

The deposition was on the edge of town, on the 3rd floor of a Chase bank building. It wasn't the prosecuting attorney's offices, but I assume the offices belonged to some attorney somewhere. I was still at the stage where I hated having to wear a suit. Having to sit through what I expected to be a massive waste of time made my tie feel especially tight.

Bill was waiting for us in the lobby. We took the elevator together and entered an office that was vacant and dark, making us feel like we were there illicitly. Waiting for us in a conference room were the opposing counsel and Mrs. Brooks, Henry's building manager. We introduced ourselves. No one but Bill had any desire to be there.

I had never been to a deposition before, and it started exactly like I had seen on television. I sat between Bill and Nathan, trying to remember to sit up straight. Mrs. Brooks and Bill would be doing almost all of the talking. Mrs. Brooks gave identifying information and opposing counsel briefly questioned her about the eviction. It was very by-the-book in that Henry was supposed to pay rent and he hadn't paid rent, and this had gone on for about six months.

Then, it was Bill's turn.

Bill stood up and proceeded to craft a labyrinthine path through Henry's history at the building, encircling all of his relations with other tenants, and his life as Mrs. Brooks knew it. Bill wanted to get every fact he could on record, for some sick reason. Meanwhile, the only disclosure I was interested in was Justin telling Gary about Ella and the weed.

Bill droned on. Expanding his scope of questions, Bill mentioned: Henry's century of backpay, Henry's tradition of using the oven to heat his apartment, and even, somehow, Bill's own personal history as a football player. Why opposing counsel let this go on, we'll never know. Perhaps she was entertained, or afraid, or maybe so numbed from these small-town lawyer exchanges that she just couldn't be bothered.

Bill honed-in on one complaint about Henry from two years prior.

"Could you describe the complaint in your own words?" Bill asked, insistent against poor Mrs. Brooks, like this was the O.J. case times ten.

"Sure," she said. Having managed public housing for 6 years, she'd seen it all. We could've come to the deposition wearing clown makeup and she wouldn't have batted an eye.

"It was about two or two fifteen in the morning." Mrs. Brooks made an effort to recall details. She was savvy enough to understand that if she didn't, Bill would ask her to specify. "I received a call from Henry's next-door neighbor—"

"Next door? What does that mean? Which neighbor?"

There was specificity, then there was this. Bill would say he was building a bulwark against the floods of misinformation; I would say he was sandbagging. I

Seat Open

wondered if he was actually an agent of entropy dragging us toward his goal of chaos. What else would he bring into question simply because he could? There was no shot clock on the table.

"Apartment 6C," said Mrs. Brooks.

"What time did Apartment 6C call?"

"I said that. About two or two-fifteen."

"Ah-ha! No, you told us when you received the call, not if they had been calling prior or—"

Bill looked like he caught her in the middle of a lie.

"Okay. That's when they called me." Mrs. Brooks described going out and seeing Henry riding his bike the length of the hallway.

"How long was the hallway?"

"About twenty feet."

"About twenty feet? That could be five feet, that could be fifty feet. What kind of measurement are you using?"

A ball of tension was building in what I thought was my solar plexus. Was this an ulcer? Maybe I could get lucky and my heart would explode in my chest. I called upon an old reliable for the second time that day—my poker face—and stared with concerned disinterest at the center of the table.

"I think it was about twenty feet." By now even Mrs. Brooks had grown cold, struck by the pettiness.

"Nathan, stand up."

Nathan, who I had forgotten was next to me, snapped out of a daze and stood up robotically. I tensed. I didn't know there would be audience participation.

"Walk until Mrs. Brooks tells you to stop," Bill directed. Nathan hesitated for a moment but, with no other option, walked alongside the conference table.

"Stop," Mrs. Brooks said. Nathan froze in place. I silently asked myself if I wouldn't be tempted to walk right on out of the room.

"Now how far would you say that is?"

If Mrs. Brooks added a drop of sarcasm, it went unnoticed.

"About twenty feet."

The deposition went on like this for two and a half hours.

Afterwards, I dropped Nathan off and bee-lined back to Justin's where we called Ella and got high. Everything was an echo of the night before— the pizza delivery, the order of the pipe, the omission of Gary. I complained about the afternoon and the pointlessness of it all. They had similar stories of witnessed ineptitudes. Drunk lawyers, adulterous judges. The more we learned about the law, the more lawless it seemed.

I thought about the vacation Bill would be going on soon. He'd escape the upcoming trial, which would be something between a circus and an execution. Henry's case had been a nightmare from the onset. An exercise in patience and foolishness. Henry would be, without a doubt, evicted from his apartment and there was nothing we could do. But it wasn't all bad. Henry had steady employment, at least for the time being. Furthermore, one of the parishioners was boarding Henry, so his housing was taken care of. The state had failed him, but maybe the church would be his salvation.

With this justification, and the usual prospect of desert riches, I skipped the trial and flew to Las Vegas the day after the deposition.

Any trepidation, guilt, or shame was quickly mitigated by remembering Bill's legal gymnastics, one after another, from his brain otherwise filled with fantasies of blinking slot reels. My departure wouldn't have been a big deal, but I was the most familiar with the case, and I'd be expected to help Bill's attorney-friend through the trial. Hopefully Nathan had paid attention.

Seat Open

I told Justin about my plans. The tournament I would play in Vegas. But we both knew the bigger draw was leaving Illinois. Justin shook his head in disapproval and drove me to the airport.

I flew into Vegas the night before the trial, leaving Bill a voicemail giving some roundabout excuse—"personal issues." I didn't feel bad, seeing as he was two hundred miles farther from the courthouse than I was. Maybe if I explained the stakes, he'd understand. I texted Nathan wishing him luck and consoling him that none of this was his fault.

Just before the plane picked up off the tarmac, I felt a pang of remorse, but otherwise I was floating above the clouds. In Vegas, my taxi pulled up to the poker house where most of my friends were living. They were barbecuing near the cabana, passing around a joint by the pool. They cheered when I walked into the backyard. Instantly, I felt I made the right decision.

The next day I was a poker player again. Thoughts of the law were for someone else. The Rio was as we had left it: scorching hot parking lot, freezing cold poker tables.

In the Amazon Room, Mike B.'s $25,000 tournament filled the area around the Thunderdome. It was populated by a who's who of professional poker players. Some celebrities and rich whales registered while they were in town and the field had ended up being quite soft.

Mike rocketed up the chip rankings with some early good play. There were only a few hundred players who entered, and they neared the money bubble. 25 players remained with 16 getting paid a minimum of $80,000. First prize was just over one million dollars.

I was nervous and didn't want to sit at home checking updates, or worse sit at the Rio, so I went to the movies and saw *Chef*. In the dark, I prided myself on resisting the temptation to check on Mike. As soon as I stepped foot

Blockhead

outside of the theatre, I opened up my PokerNews app to see the chip standings. He had busted. Eighteenth. The loss wore on Mike heavily, wanting to bring victory back to the house and his friends.

My tournament was the next day. I sold off shares, hedging my investment in myself. Even in poker, connections are important, and I was fortunate to sell pieces when better players would've had a harder time. I arrived a few hours into play, eager to skip the inconsequential early levels.

Dreams of a deep run filled my head. As I got to the Rio, I realized the trial had already occurred. I texted Nathan asking how it went. He said Bill's attorney friend had forgotten to show up. With no actual attorney to represent Henry, who also hadn't appeared, the opposing counsel asked that the case be continued. Bill would have to represent Henry sometime in September. None of it had mattered.

"Good work," I texted Nathan.

I sat down at a table with only six players and was immediately out of my element. I remembered—I wasn't a tournament player. Everyone else at my table was wearing World Poker Tour hoodies and Nike sweatpants. They had been hardened by a long summer. The swings of a tournament pro could only be handled by the criminally insane.

I was soon witness to the vicious quickness of tournaments. My stack was reduced to only a few blinds. I was all in with mediocre holdings—pocket sevens—and lost to a premium hand, busting just hours after I had parked. Standing from my seat, I had the same uncomfortable feeling that came with every tournament bust—suddenly being a bystander in your own parade.

I hurried to the rail, past the cashier, out of the giant room the tournament was held and into the hallway. Serendipity hit and I ran into friends just outside. They were a group of high stakes tournament pros I was fortunate to fall in with a few years prior. One of them was Jimmy.

An aside about Jimmy, he was known in the poker world for two things— he was the 19 year old who became an instant millionaire by finishing 2nd in an Australian poker tournament, and he was also rejected from a sponsorship with Full Tilt Poker. In an e-mail leaked throughout the poker community, the CEO of Full Tilt had called Jimmy a "freak and weird dude." Jimmy owned the phrase and used it in his bio.

Jimmy was lying on the floor, which made him a bit of a spectacle, but in the gambling world spectacle wasn't ever the problem.

"What's wrong?" I asked.

"Jimmy busted the $2,500 Stud 8 event," a friend answered.

"Life sucks," Jimmy cried out from the floor.

Without needing to explain, I lied down next to Jimmy on the hallway of the Rio. I put my head on the stubby carpet, covered with crumbs and crushed dreams. I tried to find some blamelessness in missing nonexistent Henry's case to lose a tournament, but still felt guilty. Though, it helped that even by skipping trial to fly across the country to play poker I was maybe only the second biggest degenerate in our three-person clinic. That had to count for something.

I had once heard that poker was a battle of narratives— imposing your reality on the other players. Manifesting your fortune. Hoping that was the case, I closed my eyes and mentally willed Henry all of my good luck and Bill's luck, too. He would need it.

Inheritance

Ali and I circled the roof of the Wynn's parking garage a third time when my father called. I was back in Vegas on winter break from law school. It was the week before New Year's Eve 2014 and every Californian tourist had driven in to lose their Christmas money. The phone buzzed and I rejected the call. We had lunch plans, but it was already eight o'clock. I had blown him off. It ran in the family. Nonetheless, I was a black sheep. Poker, not blackjack. Winning, not losing.

We circled the garage a fourth time. A group of European tourists strolled from the elevator, pulling luggage behind them. We followed them to a mini-van and watched them load their things without a care in the world. Clearly not losers in the slot machines, bags overloaded with luxury shopping and cheap souvenirs.

Their speed was agonizing. Ali and I waited in the car, compounding the pre-existing anxiety that came before every poker session. The Wynn loomed over us. The building was wide, concave and copper-colored. High in the air, Steve Wynn's two-story signature burned in neon on the side of his building. The tourists finally left. We bypassed the elevator and took the stairs to the casino floor.

We passed the Ferrari store where I hadn't seen anyone ever actually purchase a Ferrari but had seen several mid-forty's men walk out wearing brand-new Ferrari jackets. I liked to think that the casinos knew almost no one would ever buy a car at one of these stores, but they must've made the cost of a Formula 1 car selling merchandise alone. Casinos knew how to flourish in the desert, using every part of the buffalo.

Ali and I met Shane in front of the poker room. Shane was one of the few professional poker players who treated

Seat Open

the game like a job. Shane had been having a good year, and I was happy for him because he deserved it. He studied religiously, showed up to the casino at pre-arranged times. Shane packed lunch. That work ethic had eluded me even in my sharpest days. I had to imagine this was partially fueled by a dog and girlfriend, as well as his nineteen year-old son. Shane was thirty, the oldest member of our group. He had seen a lot.

That night we'd be taking it easy. We signed up for the lowest stakes the Wynn had to offer. Shane and Ali had already locked up their year, and I was only there to have something to do—to not be eating with my dad. No one saw any reason for the stress of higher stakes. We didn't want to tempt fate.

Shane and I were sat at the same table. I shuffled and reshuffled three small towers of five-dollar reds and one-dollar blues. I tossed out my small blind. The dealer tossed my change back to me and the chips barely touched the felt before I added them to my stacks. I was comforted by the nonverbal back and forth. The ballet that existed between regulars and dealers. As the dealer pitched the cards, I felt an immediate connection. I missed this at law school—they talked too much there.

I turned the cards sideways and peeled back the top corners to see them both—rank and suit. When I hadn't been playing cards for a long time, my thumb would get calloused every first day back. Someone raised and I folded my hand.

I felt unavoidable nostalgia, like a family reunion held at the same house every year. I had played a lot of poker, and when I dreamt about playing it was often at the Wynn. I tried to do some old chip tricks. With nothing else to do, you can't help but end up competent at rolling porcelain discs around your knuckles.

I made small talk with Shane when a man who I termed "Life Coach" sat at the table. Life Coach looked like Orson

Blockhead

Welles if Orson Welles had been a vegan in 1970s Burbank, tracksuit and all. I had played with him the day before. He earned his name when, after witnessing me get beaten in a particularly brutal series of hands, he said, "You took that like a man. Good. Always stay positive." He said this with a big, fat smile. I was happy to see him.

But his happy disposition was replaced with the familiar look of a troubled gambler. A worriedness I usually saw in one of the shittier casinos. If not worried, sad. He was wearing the same clothes as yesterday. He took a phone call and spoke softly enough that I couldn't hear him across the table. His voice remained even the entire time. He hung up. Finally, he said, "Boy, I better not find out who gave my wife my cell phone number." He tossed out a smile and I was relieved he was playing along. I checked my phone. Another message from dad. Deleted.

Shane leaned over and whispered, "This is a good game."

There was a mythos in poker culture akin to "Head West, young man" – the search for the "good game." Generally, it followed as such: A game would be good at a certain casino and everyone would flock there. Said game was then no longer good and the players stewed in their mediocre games until rumors of another "good game" emerged. This cycle repeated forever.

I told Shane that all the games looked good and he smiled and nodded and voiced his agreement.

A plump, mustachioed Dealer sat down, and I noticed his name tag—Cowboy.

"Is that your real name?" another player asked.

"Yup," Cowboy said, matter-of-factly. "And my last name's Boots."

I laughed out loud despite the fact that Cowboy had probably told that joke more times than I'd played poker.

A very large man took a seat to my right. He wasn't necessarily fat, just built with bigger pieces than anyone

Seat Open

else. Behind him, a lithe blonde woman rolled a chair over to spectate. Her air of confidence and Louis Vuitton bag (and the absence of a ring on either of them) told me we weren't the only professionals at the table.

"Did I bring my charger?" he asked her.

"It's in the room, Ned."

"Goddamnit."

I noticed Ned's watch was worth more than everyone's chip stacks combined. I quickly volunteered my charger.

There is a rule in gambling culture: "Don't loan what you don't mind losing." But that rule is trumped by another rule: "Don't tap the (fish)tank." The more money a fish indicates you can win off them, the more acquiescent you should be. That could mean drinking. It could also mean agreeing with the fish's opinion on the weather, movies, the Yankees pitching rotation, or American foreign policy. Not overtly agreeing but acknowledging as totally valid.

It also meant staring at your chips when the fish berated the dealer for an unlucky card while calling her a stupid bitch and threatening to have her fired. To have a problem with a fish was to have a problem with your money. I pulled out my phone charger and offered it to the man named Ned. I apologized for having an older model.

"Perfect," he said, showing me he had the same phone.

"Aren't we a little behind the times?" I asked.

"Bullshit. The latest technology is for women, midgets, and orphans."

Welcome to the table, Ned.

Ned immediately brought up his Wharton MBA.

"You look identical to my favorite professor—that guy pretty much ran Wharton."

He showed me a picture on his charging phone: an 85 year old Jewish man with islands of wispy white hair.

"Don't you see it?" Ned gave the prompting look of a guy who usually got what he wanted. He must've played football at the collegiate level. Probably at a position that allowed him maximum collisions. I remembered the rule—don't tap the tank.

"We could be twins," I told Ned.

Ned said he was a vice president of a company I had never heard of, and he never got around to specifying what they did before he interrupted himself. His date was scrolling through pictures on her phone. Ned looked over her shoulder and saw something that made the Wharton graduate, vice president, captain of industry, shout, "What the fuck!"

"That's the ugliest fuckin' thing I've seen in my life." Ned said. "No cheesesteak should be made with provolone."

"Baby, c'mon."

"No. I'm from Philly. I know."

I was certain I had fine enough cheesesteaks with provolone, but I would rather lose a finger than tell Ned as much.

"Any good cheesesteak is topped with cheese whiz from a big vat spooned out by an African American man."

I looked to the one black kid at the table, a few seats over. Because of his constant raises, a thorn in my side, I had pegged him as decent player. He didn't react to Ned's comment. His headphones were in, but he was there to make money, so it wasn't clear that he hadn't heard Ned.

Ned's date laughed and called him an asshole, and he reiterated cheesesteak canon with a timbre in his voice that denoted the end of the conversation. I looked at Shane to see if he had anything to say, but he was also zoned out, nodding to his own headphones. Silence fell and Ned's words became cheesesteak law.

A cocktail waitress dropped off a pineapple juice for me. Whenever I played, even when I was drinking, I ordered one. There was something undeniable about drinking pineapple juice in the desert. One hundred years ago, there was nothing but sand and Joshua trees. Now, anything you

Seat Open

wanted. Where was the closest pineapple? Hawaii? Central America? The only thing nature grew in Las Vegas was scorpions.

Ned asked me what I did, and I said I went to law school. He said he had a law degree which given his A-type personality and psychotic statements didn't surprise me. I didn't tell him that I regretted my decision every day, nor did I tell him I didn't actually plan on practicing law. I reveled in the slight respect I got from being a law student, even though the hardest part had been getting accepted.

Ned didn't play many hands, other than calling some raises and folding. He played conservatively, there was no heart in it. He was bored. They both were. The stakes weren't high enough. Ned's date, whose name I never learned, stood up. She told Ned to be at the room in fifteen minutes. He said he would, and she asked me that, if he didn't leave, to force him away. I knew I couldn't, but I also wouldn't have to. After fifteen minutes, Ned unplugged his phone, wishing me good luck and reaffirming I made the right decision going to law school. My phone alerted me it was dying. No more missed calls from dad. His last voicemail likely said to come by on my way home and we could get Burger King. He didn't know I was around the corner. He lived near a rundown local's casino called the Gold Coast, in a house that was actually his mother's house. He didn't even know I played cards. I could've stopped by, but I wouldn't.

Shane changed tables for another "good game" and as the night wound down, two men took the newly opened seats to my left. They were unmistakably father and son. Speaking Farsi, they were probably from Iran, like my father. I couldn't understand what they were saying because I never learned the language. Under the dad's salt and pepper crown, his soft features betrayed leisure over hard work. I guessed he was an academic or engineer of some kind. His son wore a puffy North Face jacket even though it was seventy degrees outside and had a haircut that could only be described as "shorn," and in fact was what made me guess they were from the old country to begin with.

They greeted me with curt nods and full smiles. Their body language was relaxed, though they had a way of sitting, leaning in together, that was almost conspiratory. It was us against them.

Their first hand, the father called a bet and three cards were laid out out across the middle of the table. The father squinted to see them. His son told him something in Farsi and the dealer reprimanded them.

"English only at the table."

The son immediately apologized. He was just telling his dad the cards, he explained with an accented English that reminded me of cousins I hadn't seen in a decade. The father folded and waved to the table, apologizing for any misgivings, saying he was getting old with a regretful smile. He was forgiven.

The father bled away his chips, mostly calling and calling and calling, a glaring sign of an amateur player. Regardless, they made kind small talk, and were probably two of the most unaggressive people I had seen at the table that day at a game that is fundamentally confrontational.

At one point, the father was down from his initial $300 buy-in to his last $100. His son maintained his initial stack, taking a more conservative playstyle. I picked up Ace / King, a good hand, and raised $15. The father called. Just the two of us remained.

We were dealt a flop of nine, eight, three. I checked and the father shoved all of his chips in and I meekly folded, oddly relieved about the whole thing. The son slapped the table and said, "Way to go, Dad!" with a sincerity that was refreshing. He even smiled at me afterwards, the loser of the hand, because why wouldn't I be happy, too? And still up a few hundred for the day, I was.

Seat Open

The next hand I had two Jacks and a bad feeling. I raised $10 and the father re-raised to $30. I called and the board came ten, seven, three. I checked and he checked. I was still awash in the afterglow of a rare moment of human decency at the poker table.

The turn brought a nine, and I checked and he checked again. I figured he probably didn't have much and would give up the hand to any aggression. The river was an eight giving me a straight; Seven-through-Jack and before I could think the father moved all-in with his last $100.

The official table rule was that since I hadn't acted and the Father had bet behind me, I had two possible options: First, I could bet and take over the action, negating his errant all-in. Meaning, I could bet $20 trying to signal to this man that I had a very good hand, almost certainly the best hand, and that he should only call and save his money, and more importantly the pride in his son's eyes, and how once that's gone, it's gone, so please be careful gambling it.

The second option was to check and let the bet stand. I would likely win the pot, and end his night.

I made eye contact with the dealer and said, loud enough to be heard clearly, "Check." The bet stood. I then tossed out a single $5 chip indicating a call. I wouldn't be putting any more of my chips in—they weren't moving.

The father excitedly rolled over two eights for a worthless three of a kind. It had to be explained by his son, twice, once in Farsi, why he didn't win the pot and why his chips were going to me. He may not have understood the hand, but he understood that he lost. The father solemnly nodded and reached over to slide half of his son's chips in front of him to continue playing. This was a cardinal "don't" in poker, but I was the only one that noticed, and I pretended like I didn't.

The father and son bickered, and I could only imagine it was because the kid had been playing tight since they got there and still had his chips and the dad was burning their

Blockhead

money. I stood up, got a chip rack, and cashed out. I didn't want to play anymore.

I was distraught. I found Ali and Shane seated together.

"I feel really bad about taking this guy's money," I said to both of them. Either of them. This feeling wasn't familiar in all my time playing cards. Shane didn't turn away from his table and Ali looked at me, blankly.

"That's a sentence you will never hear me say."

I watched Ali and Shane play for about an hour. At three in the morning, we left. On the way to our favorite sushi spot, we passed the Gold Coast and my father's house. I barely turned my head as we sped by, anxious to get food.

I hadn't eaten all day.

ICON

Late November, 2017

Day 2
Price of ICX: $0.25

I rode in an Uber to a beach house where I was staying for an indefinite amount of time. I had $40 in my bank account and thousands of dollars in cryptocurrency.

Bitcoin had taken off. Most of our poker group had been made aware of the digital currency when the DOJ shut down online poker and were forced to rely on bitcoin or teams of poker player-agents in Asia, like a Millennial dropout hawala network. By early-2017, there was an undeniable "crypto" buzz in most poker circles. I had picked up online poker again and bought bitcoin, needing to deposit funds. But while I won money playing poker, I was profiting more from the appreciation of the bitcoin. I jumped one runaway train for another. I asked around. Of course, Ben was in the know.

After a few weeks, I quit my job because I was making more trading cryptocurrency in my spare time. In this bull market, a syphilitic monkey could get rich. By August, our friend JT came to Ben (and me, by proxy) with an investment opportunity. Hype was surrounding a new coin launching in South Korea, and we had connections that could get us in to the private presale. I asked about the coin. JT responded over Telegram message with a shiny, prestigious sounding name— ICON.

I asked JT to describe the coin and he said three words: Korean scam play. That was all I needed to hear. The general public was in a frenzy for all things crypto and this had the potential to take off, possibly returning ten or twenty times my investment. I went all in for every spare dollar I had—only a few hundred at the time. We were allowed into a private investment round for 11 cents per coin and had allegedly already doubled our money by the time the public sale was available. We were overjoyed.

Ben lived at the beach house with JT, where I could conveniently wait out the storm of my decisions. Both of them were vacationing internationally, so our friend Alan was housesitting. He was excited for me to come—insistent almost. He joked that the house, idyllic in its isolation—was so out of reach it felt like a space station. He was a lone astronaut in orbit.

Alan was one of my best friends and fit in well within the poker group for his easygoing attitude. Alan was depressed in a way that could've been mitigated, I thought, with greater purpose. I pressed him on his interests, but he never broached further than listening to EDM, watching sports, and hating everything else, including whatever job he was working at the time. At the moment, he was a bartender. He was supportive to a fault.

I was going to keep him company. His only real duty was watching Morty, a stray dog JT had adopted before leaving. Despite having a studio apartment twenty minutes away, Alan cut his lease and effectively moved into the house. It was erratic behavior, but normalized by the fact that Alan had three times as much invested into ICON as I did. If I had all my chips in, he had bet the potato farm.

Real estate became a problem one block away from the beach, and houses shared a single, private alley giving access to their cars and tucked away front doors. I wasn't sure of the address, but I knew the house from the Audi R8 parked in the driveway. It was covered in dust, engine likely seized since it hadn't been driven in over a year. Cobwebs peaked from under the tires. I wasn't sure which of my friends owned it. Waste not, want not.

Seat Open

I texted Alan and he opened the garage, greeting me. I surveyed the lay of the land. There was a giant kitchen with a marble island open to a living room where the TV, a giant L-couch, and computer desks (read: Wal-Mart folding tables) were. Naturally, that was where Alan and I would spend most of our time trading cryptocurrency and gambling, effectively the same thing. There was a second living room where JT would've spent most of his time, and instead Morty spent the days napping on his own sofa. The life of a poker dog was unparalleled luxury.

There was dog hair along all the walls that must have taken months to accumulate considering Morty wasn't very big. The trash always seemed full and despite the fact that everyone was a homebody, it lacked any sort of "homey" feel. The house would've been considered messy if not for the total lack of things. Ben and JT rented it furnished over a year ago and had another six months on the lease. It doubled as a summer house during vacation season which just meant they paid three times the rent to not bother moving out those months.

I took a spare mattress in a loft. Alan came up and we vocalized our worry about ICX and its viability. Alan had invested so much, because he was trying to jumpstart something in his life. I knew his story, because it was also my story. His parents were degenerates, stuck in their desert town. He needed a big win to get out. There had been some close calls in poker but this, he thought, could be his shot. I selfishly thought it could be his shot, too.

Day 3
ICX Price: $0.75

I woke up early, never much for sleep. I checked on Morty who fed off Alan's energy and laid around the couch, lost in a general fugue state.

Blockhead

I started every day checking the price of ICX on my phone. I saw we were up 7x our investment and my heart raced. What started as a small investment was rapidly ballooning to a larger portion of my net worth. There was a single problem. Until the company released our tokens, we couldn't sell and actualize their value. We couldn't dump them on bigger idiots. We were trapped playing a high stakes game of musical chairs.

I went to the rooftop patio to enjoy a joint and fresh air. Despite being two blocks away, I could only make out a sliver of the ocean between neighboring chimneys. The cold air was nice and woke me up. People worked their whole lives for this, and I was given it. I took advantage and brought the joint to the beach.

Highway 1 was just starting to become a major commuter artery with leased BMWs and C-Class Benzes throttling toward Los Angeles. I crossed and as I approached the ocean, an unconscious smile crept on my face. It is always a beautiful sight to see infinite land meeting infinite water. I thought of a woman I knew who skydived three times a week. She told me it was important for human beings to see the horizon and be put in perspective as animals. She was right.

I stood on the beach for what felt like an adequate amount of time getting high and staring at the water until all my anxieties cooled, if not dissipated completely.

In the afternoon, Alan and I ordered donuts from a nearby bakery— Donuttery. We ordered deep fried churro donuts, peanut butter and jelly-filled, and, our favorite, malasadas—Portuguese donuts coated with cinnamon filled with vanilla bean or guava. We chased whatever dopamine we could to keep the anxiety at bay. Alan and I speculated what we'd do the next day.

"Do you think we'll get our coins?" Alan asked.

The eternal question. I told him we could probably expect our coins by Christmas with all the hope of a boy

Seat Open

writing to Santa. I considered how paying $30 (after tip) for a dozen "artisan donuts" didn't seem to be great investment advice, but it was at least no worse than gambling on pretend internet money.

However, when the pretend internet money kept doubling in value, what else were you supposed to do but buy frivolous shit?

Day 9
ICX Price: $1.10

Alan and I had our days down to a formula.

In the mornings, I woke up and checked the price and news that occurred since I went to sleep, four hours prior. I went to the beach and meditated on what was out of my hands. Back at the house, I would do some work until Alan came down, and we spent the rest of the day getting high. Alan would make us acai or avocado wraps—a master of both from his juice shop beat.

Alan played music on the house's sound system and watched sports, while I wrote and traded. This went on most of the day, when we weren't ordering food or talking about what to order. We cooked occasionally, but Alan and I were both quick to justify delivery as a preemptive reward system being the lazy degenerates we were.

Alan was right. We were in a space station. Our closest friends were an hour away and while our phones told us we were rich, we couldn't spend our ICX coins on airfare for a real vacation. We were having a bad time in a great place. We were in a Bret Easton Ellis version of *Moon*.

The problem was we were hyper-conscious of our formulaic days and our execution of them. In the pursuit of stimulation, we'd walk to get groceries or take Morty to the beach. We'd end our nights driving out to Chitpotle or somewhere nearby for dinner, possibly getting delivery again—maybe Donuttery—and smoked until we felt like sleeping. There's a thin line between Heaven and Hell.

Day 14
ICX Price: $1.50

The difference between weekend and weekdays became cosmetic.

Within our routines, I had my own set of private mini-routines for preserving my sanity. I hadn't seen my therapist in weeks. To replace her, I started going to the corner store and picking up a large blue raspberry ICEE every day. This was on top of the ounce of marijuana Alan and I were smoking every two days. Sweet, then smokey. My mouth was stained blue.

Some days, that corner store was the only place I went. It was the nicest version of a bodega I'd ever seen with a Boar's Head delicatessen built-in. They even had a walk-in humidor. This was how the other half lived.

The clientele was shaken out of a checkout aisle romance novel. Women in large, flat-brimmed hats and sundresses. Men permanently wearing open Tommy Bahamas shirts with no intention of ever leaving nor going to the beach.

When it was raining—which thankfully had only been a handful of withering days—Alan and I were forced inside to succumb to the same Soundcloud playlists on repeat. Him rolling joints while I checked the price, checked the news, then checked the price again. Restlessness trickled into the house. All Alan and I could do was wait until JT or Ben sent us our coins.

Alan ordered a 5,000-piece puzzle. He believed it would pass the time faster. I considered this was how prison inmates or lonely octogenarians spent their unyielding days. Maybe a puzzle was a way of patching together a fractured relationship with God. I thought that's what the ICEE was for.

Day 19
ICX Price: $2.15

Panic hit when the price spiked to almost $2, then plunged to a weekly low of $0.75. We stayed glued to Twitter where anonymous accounts with avatars of cartoon animals discussed up-to-the-minute market trends and rumored inside information. These cartoon characters were often connected to development teams or incredibly wealthy market makers.

Fundamental and technical analysis was meted out, argued over back-and-forth to the point of mundanity, stacking pointlessness upon pointlessness. We only liked and retweeted the posts that said we would be rich.

Despite my trading profits (being constantly eaten away by delivery expenses) existence felt like it was chained to our ICX holdings. They had more mass than I did. I simply gravitated around them, hoping to be granted clearance to dock. We ordered more weed.

Day 28
ICX Price: $4.45

Our puzzle arrived in the mail.

Five thousand pieces and Alan, unbeknownst to me, had ordered a wickedly difficult underwater landscape. Other than schools of multicolored fish, 70% of the puzzle was the same deep, ocean blue. It was like Alan was trying to crush our spirits. But he didn't seem concerned, and sure enough, set to work building the puzzle's border. I helped where I could, but mostly focused on the bits of coral and fish—the easiest parts. My back quickly got sore hunched over the table, so I stopped. Alan was driven.

The rain clouds receded so I went to the miniature outdoor courtyard where a hot tub Alan and I never used sat filled with tepid water. I stared at it, feeling guilty, wondering if anything had time to grow before the gardeners cleaned it. I wondered what day it was, because I hadn't seen them around in a while. I went back in and helped Alan with the puzzle.

It was about 5PM that night while we were ordering dinner with terribly limited options that I realized— it was Christmas.

Day 31
ICX Price: $4.82

ICX hit prices we never thought possible. Euphoria hit. Alan and I spent a stupid amount of time every day calculating how much money we made. For some reason, I got a job.

A mutual poker friend, impressed I knew so much about the crypto industry due to my forced obsession, offered me a job working remotely for an app. It consisted primarily of low-level marketing and answering e-mails, and I was ecstatic to have something to do.

The ICON team announced they were releasing a wallet. This was more or less meaningless as our tokens still hadn't been released. Still, the price pumped; there was an entire community of people made rich by this coin, awaiting their wealth, creating an echo chamber of positivity. It was dangerous.

Day 36
ICX Price: $8.15

I paid rent on an apartment I hadn't seen in a month. A tiny sum in comparison to what my investment had blossomed into. We continued spending frivolously. Ben

Seat Open

sent Alan housesitting money and some petty cash to live off of. Alan had less than $100 in the bank, but his investment was worth almost six figures.

Alan and I downloaded the newest ICX wallet. It was sleek but had almost no features and presented us with a giant stylized 0. I ran through a routine of checking Twitter, Reddit, and every major crypto news outlet. I checked news updates like a mad man. I blamed it on getting accustomed to my new job.

The ICON team was having a launch event. Termed the "Genesis Summit", they were renting out the nicest office building in Seoul and hosting several VIPs and whales, including JT.

Alarm bells rang in my head. We were getting returns people only dreamed about. 80x our investment. These were the unsustainable heights. A group of people could have created a new coin in under thirty minutes branded off their favorite TV show and raised a ten-million-dollar market cap in a few days. In fact, that exact thing happened. A few times.

Day 42
ICX Price: $12.20

Every day the price jumped higher on anticipation of the Summit conference. Finally, there was a reprieve: stopping on his way to Seoul, JT came home. I wasn't sure what to expect. While Alan and I made thousands, JT had made millions. We did some quick calculations once and figured he was sitting on 8 figures worth of ICON. If we felt anxious, he must've felt psychotic.

But JT was incredibly relaxed almost to the point of coldness. When I woke up and went downstairs, he was happily petting Morty, working at his computer. As a tactful reminder, one of the first things he did was complain he was unable to sell right now, he had no access to the tokens. That set the tone immediately, and we commiserated about our frozen coins together.

But JT reminded me about what was important.

"We're rich now," he said.

JT made it feel real. He seemed quite happy and didn't think the whole thing could fall to zero, which greatly concerned me. I told him to enjoy his trip to Seoul and he thanked me without bothering to look away from his monitor.

Day 45
ICX Price: $8.40

Alan and I were certain it was over.

The price blew off near $12 and had fallen just under double digits. Still a massive gain for us, but we were panicked at the 30% drop and tens of thousands of dollars collectively wiped off the table between us. We had to sell.

Every day brought new stomachaches. Fear and anticipation were the base elements in my gut. It became clear to me that we were no longer waiting for the price to rise or our fortunes to grow—we were trying to get out alive. As the story goes, the dream was collapsing.

Alan and I hit a wall with the puzzle. We pieced together all of the easy sections and now spent hours moving, piece-by-piece, fitting, turning, fitting again. It wasn't uncommon to spend two or three hours at the puzzle table before tapping out, not adding a single piece to the mass. Those moments were especially disheartening, wasting time for the sheer sake of it.

I considered how lucky we were to have a "puzzle table" in a beach town in Southern California, even if we weren't making any progress. People paid thousands for that much space in a month. I checked the price again. We had lost months of rent in hours.

Seat Open

Day 51
ICX Price: $11.01

The price bounced and the group was instantly euphoric again. The roller coaster went on. Alan's tab of borrowed spending money breached four figures. It was Ancient Rome—Nero, not Caesar.

Time moved slower. Alan and I were on-edge knowing full well our phones could buzz at any moment telling us we would have our money, or we were poor again. It was thrilling. None of it felt real and yet it was impossible to ignore. Our group chat talked about $50 or $100 ICX.

"What if it went up just another 5x? Or 10x? Could you imagine?"

How much bigger could a bubble get, I wondered?

There were already rumblings on the ground, large beasts approaching, oncoming danger. Some of the more obvious scam coins were being looked at by regulators and the entire industry was seen as dumb money. An article titled "Everyone is Getting Hilariously Rich and You're Not" showed up in the New York Times, detailing the craziness of overnight wealth. Alan and I discussed the accuracy of the article. Less Lambos, more lambs.

Talking about money so much, I couldn't help but probe: what were Alan's plans when we got paid? He rattled off a list of small debts, including money owed to me, and then assured me the brunt of his investment would go to a future. What future, I wasn't sure, but it would be a good apartment somewhere happier.

We took Alan's car the half mile to the store, rather than walked. But when we loaded back in with our snacks and juices, the engine wouldn't turn. If we wanted a message, we got one. This was the bottom.

Alan had the expected freak-out. He punched his window and yelled at fate. Really, who could blame him? I tried to console him. In a matter of days, he'd be able to buy a new car. Whatever he wanted. An Audi to match JT's. A Tesla to match Ben's. We walked back together to the house, while Alan cooled off, and I quietly downed my ICEE. I assuaged him with future of a Hollywood Hills apartment, rent paid for the year.

Day 58
ICX Price: $9.10

One day before the Summit.

JT was gone, but Ben was back in town and stayed at the house, providing some semblance of balance. Later that night, Ben informed us that JT had arrived at the Summit, it was morning in Korea, and he was completely drinking the Kool-Aid.

There were multiple development teams launching their "decentralized apps" on the ICON network and even vending machines taking ICX tokens on-site. JT was convinced ICX had another 5x to climb. We would be much, much richer.

Alan, a man on a mission, asked if our tokens were released and sellable yet. Ben said no. But, he said, JT was willing to buy anyone's allocation for 90% of its current value. This was it. Our escape pod home.

I looked at Alan and told him we had to sell. I checked the group chat where Ben gave everyone the same offer and extended my advice to all of our friends. I wasn't a market genius, nor was I even sure why I was selling, but I knew that no one was going to buy our eleven-cent coins from us for much more than ten dollars. It just didn't make sense.

The group chat had a different belief and was talking about a month-long AirBnB stay in Amsterdam once the price hit $25. They had found a house with an entire room made of beanbags. To me, this just confirmed we had to sell.

Seat Open

Alan and I told JT our plans to sell and gave him my wallet address to send the coins. Alan trusted me to make the transfers for both mine and his coins, which was both incredibly convenient and very stressful. I checked the numbers five times to make sure there were no typos.

The nature of cryptocurrency transfers was stress-ridden in itself, being completely irreversible. We were like starved prisoners waiting to be fed; we sat nodding our heads, rocking and waiting. We obsessively refreshed the webpage. Finally, without celebration, the coins showed up in my exchange wallet. I sold them off in chunks and the bitcoin poured in as buyers sucked up the liquidity. Even at $9, people were eager to buy. The Summit hype was working. The music kept playing. People kept dancing.

I couldn't help but enjoy the tens of thousands of dollars in my account. We had to wait a few days to withdrawal it all, but we were finally on our way out of the forest. I had to stop for a moment and consider if ICX wasn't really going to $50, but I knew that wasn't worth the risk. It was time to cash out.

I congratulated Alan on his big win. It finally played out like we wanted. "We did it," I told him. "I can't believe it."

Day 60
ICX Price: $7.93

As poker players, we had seen success, but that had been earned. This was different. This felt like being at the right place at the right time. There was even a small bit of schadenfreude for our friends who already lost ten percent of their holdings deciding to not sell.

I invested in more coins and cashed out to get ahead on rent. Alan was quick to celebrate, though. And by celebrate, I mean splurge. He wanted to feel the win. That weekend, Alan bought a new bong ($500), an electronic pipe implement for the bong ($299), new Steph Curry shoes ($200), Lakers floor seats ($1000), a new laptop ($2000), and a Nintendo Switch ($300).

By the time I questioned if we were spending intelligently, he was shopping for a Vespa on his new laptop. The entire thing felt like the Disney movie, *Blank Check*. Whatever impulse we had, no matter how absurd, was granted instantly. The only way we could've had less responsibility was if we wore diapers.

We ordered Donuttery three days in a row. Takeout boxes were stacked high. I thought maybe now was the time Alan would slingshot himself into a better trajectory, but the days after cashing out were bedazzled clones of the days before. Life felt like an amusement park, with just as much soft anxiety of getting lost.

Day 62
ICX Price: $5.35

Superbowl Sunday. The day when every gambler across the country bets on the most tightly handicapped game of the year.

ICON, as most of the market, was falling through the floor. What felt like fortunate timing turned out to be a lifeboat off the Titanic. Alan and I were bulwarked from destruction with cash. Our friends were down thousands, the market down billions. I didn't want to know how much JT was down. All I had managed when we made the exchange was a "thanks" and his response, "lol np," was like the cursed last words of a dead man.

But there was a leak in our lifeboat. Alan and I were still floating along on the Sea of Indulgence. The latest bout of idiocy was my decision to bet ~$5,000 on the Patriots to beat the Eagles. I had fallen into a sports-betting binge, betting small amounts on anything just to have something to root for. European basketball, Japanese golf, e-sports. Fortunately, I was mostly breaking even. Ben had already

Seat Open

left to go back to Chicago for some time and I had plans to leave soon, continuing work at the startup. That left Alan.

Alan was moving back with his parents to figure things out there. He wanted to trade cryptocurrency full-time, having caught the bug. He had a decent starting roll and accounts on the exchanges. What more did he need? But a seed of doubt grew in my stomach when he asked me which coins I thought were good buys; and, where I thought the market was going in the future? There were rumors of an extended bear market that would be vicious to anyone still investing. Somehow, Alan was undeterred.

The puzzle sat half-finished. We hadn't touched it once other people came into the house, the lone tether between our space station and our homeworld. I packed my bag. I was worried the window provided for Alan by the money would quickly shut, and I wasn't sure how to tell him to hurry out while he still could.

I felt bad for the group. They sold a good portion but what was left of their coins was barely worth half as much. The meat was rotting on the bone. Now was the time to pay the bill, not sit down. But there was nothing I could do. We didn't know the market would lose another 90% of its value.

Ben messaged us later that day saying he'd heard of two new projects— Constellation and IndieParty. They were about to launch, and like ICON, he wanted to know if we were interested in investing. He said he probably wasn't buying much, and I confirmed that was a good idea and "only" invested a few thousand. But Alan wanted more. He said he felt good, that the ride was going to continue, and he invested five figures into each. I asked if he was sure, but by his calculations, even a triple of his money would be game changing. When you're on a streak you have to bet it. Or something.

I Ubered the whole way back to Hollywood instead of taking the train like I had planned. When I got back home, I

Blockhead

saw my kitchen was infested with moths. I wasn't bothered. Money could actually solve this problem.

Seat Open

The Ruby Dragon Baccarat Championship (2016)

Building the Team

I stood on a busy Hollywood street corner with a duffle bag, looking like a lamb fresh off the bus. Like every other writer, actor, or director around me, I had a dream of riches and a plan of someone else to make it happen.

A blue, domed Honda Accord pulled up. Ben leaned out of the window.

"Let's play baccarat."

We fled the city into the California desert. Ben's friend Rodney drove on cruise control, one hairy foot hanging out the window, ponytail whipping behind him. Rodney was a friend of Ben's from high school, which meant he was a friend of mine. We were headed to Las Vegas to play in the Ruby Dragon Baccarat Championship. It was meant to sound prestigious, and it almost was.

Half promotional baccarat tournament, half lure for rich Asian flounders, Ben was taking advantage of the event by putting together a team of competent poker players, and staking them to "beat the casino" and win a lion's share of the prize pool.

After winning on Obama in 2012, Ben had continued to crush the live poker scene, even being made fun of for his resemblance to Ben Stiller during WSOP Main Event coverage on ESPN. He told us he was mocked in poker rooms around the country for the next year. We were very proud of him.

I had never played baccarat before, but Ben assured me that wouldn't be a problem. It seemed like a fairly uncomplicated game, little more than betting on coin flips.

That much I could understand. Ben had organized a "test team" the year before, with our friends Shane and Melanie. They made $15k and $60k, respectively. Shane was one of the hardest working poker pros I ever met, and Melanie was his stay-at-home girlfriend who was really more of a partner-in-crime, as those things go. A lot of their winnings went to their Shih Tzu, Doug.

Ben buzzed with excitement which was surprising because, like all great gamblers, he always had an even keel. Neither Rodney nor I knew what to expect, but I had a sleep mask and Rodney had a sandwich, which he was kind enough to share. I dozed off and didn't realize we were in Las Vegas until we were in line for hotel registration with a court jester standing on a giant multicolored ball in the middle of the lobby.

Checking In

We were staying in the Venetian, which modeled itself after the river-streets of Venice, Italy. If the Venetian would have you believe, those streets were rife with 2-for-1 $100 couture t-shirts and Japanese tourists.

Ben checked us in, then we followed him to three more hotels where we checked-in rooms for the rest of the team. Ben got a free hotel room at any Caesar's property because he was a Seven Star, the highest VIP rating given to Caesars's Rewards players. This designation, the result of some absurd amount of gambling, allowed him free cruises, shopping credits, and a room every weekday at any Caesar's property. Only the biggest whales are Seven Stars. Notably, Las Vegas mass shooter Stephen Paddock was also a Seven Star.

Starving from the drive, we walked to the Grand Lux to meet up with the rest of the team. The Grand Lux was the go-to 24/7 spot at the Venetian. It had a nine-page menu in tiny font and served everything you could ever want. The

Seat Open

Grand Lux was good, never great, large portions, and reasonably priced. Cheesecake Factory without the Cheesecake.

Joining us was Jimmy, a recognizable, old school internet poker player and his friend, Joe John. I used to read about Jimmy's poker exploits online and was lucky now to consider him a close friend. Joe John had a beard to his chest and brandished a multi-tool within two minutes of meeting him. He was a guy who stayed "off-the-grid."

At a point in the conversation he said, "I'd shoot my way out of here before I paid for any of this." He proceeded to eat a Luna Bar he brought and ordered only water.

The waiter brought out stacks of crispy, golden fried chicken and plates of avocado. We got our ducks in a row and the agenda for the next three days was explained to me.

The Ruby Dragon Baccarat Championship

The tournament was oddly like Jeopardy! There were three rounds—group play, survivor, and final. The goal was always the same: accumulate the most chips.

Group play had unlimited entries for $100 each. The top 100 places after group play finished won money, but more importantly, the top 50 spots advanced to the next round with more payouts; if you lost your chips, you bought in for $100 and went to a new table to try again. Ben came in by sponsoring every buy-in. We didn't worry about money, only advancing.

The real lure was the larger cash prizes in the later rounds of the tournament. The intent of the promotion was to draw rich Asian whales at higher stakes levels who were allowed free entry. This was a highly lucrative opportunity, especially considering Ben also paid for research of optimized betting strategies.

It made sense why Ben invested. The potential payout was staggering. After three rounds in Las Vegas, winners flew to Macau to play for millions with these illusive Chinese whales. I had visions of Scrooge McDuck swimming in his vault of coins.

We would spend most of the next week memorizing strategies, telling us when to bet and why, and running simulations. It was important to have the skills down, cold, because it was against the rules to consult any outside source, including notes or other players. More than wanting to play good baccarat, I wanted to be invited back and I didn't want to look stupid in front of my friends.

Training

Jimmy thought it would be good to get Chipotle catered to his hotel room for the first group training session. I was thankful that I was splitting a room with Ben. The scent of Chipotle permeated into the hallway on the way from the elevator. It didn't help the studying.

Despite being a competent poker pro, I had never been an especially good math player, and I was easily the worst in the group. Learning the ins-and-outs of a foreign game sometimes felt like being back in high school Chemistry, but unlike Mr. Roble's class, I kept at this. What if I had 65k chips against 45k, 30k, and 20k? How should I bet the final hand? We ran through scenarios until the correct strategies were well-tread paths in my head.

Open Play

I was incredibly high-strung all morning, having made a deal with Ben to not do any drugs until after the tournament finished. I put on a movie in the room that I didn't want to watch. It barely kept me less anxious than dead silence. When it was time to start group play, everyone met at the Venetian, and we were the first players in line, not afraid to look like what we were: a motley crew teaming up against

Seat Open

Sheldon Adelson and the Venetian Casino along with every other David armed with $100 and a slingshot.

We each bought dozens of entries with Ben's funds and watched as a line of casino staff mechanically wrote out receipts. It looked like a scene at an old-school numbers shop. We each received one free giveaway shirt. The bright yellow and red Chinese characters—good luck colors in the culture—made us look like Shanghai McDonald's executives.

We gathered around a giant Wizard of Oz MegaBucks machine, steeling ourselves for five hours of marathon baccarat. As Ben's horses in his stable, we swapped small pieces of each other's profits, trading percentages that could equate to thousands, hoping all of us wound up in Macau together.

To make sure Ben wasn't screwed, we incurred "make up." If you ran up a lot of buy-ins, you had to "make up" the difference before you saw any prize money. You didn't owe any money if you busted, but if you lost $5K in buy-ins, you had to win $5,100 before you saw profit. We were used to strict bookkeeping as poker players, despite our laid-back comradery.

While we waited for the tournament to start, other players trickled in. Mostly Asian, unsurprising. Mostly degenerates, also unsurprising. A few blessed souls wore the free shirts from last year, a more dignified purple and black.

At 10AM, our table numbers were called. I took another $500 in rebuys from Ben and found my seat. The first round of play was exclusively about amassing a chip stack to top the leaderboard presented on digital screens around the tournament area. Middle of the pack was worth zero. We played for Macau.

I sat at my first table with a group of other gamblers. We waited a few minutes, and with a proclamation from the

MC, the dealer asked for our bets. The game ran just like practice.

I don't mean the cards come out in a certain pattern, or time flew by, but I won every hand.

Every bonus, every tie, all of my player/bank bets. I won nine hands in a row.

On the tenth and final hand, I bet the maximum, again, and lost. It didn't matter, my run was so pure the dealer congratulated me and knew, for certain, that I would be advancing. I was stunned. It couldn't be that easy. But when I turned to face my friends, they looked defeated. They explained to me that, because of how statistically improbable my run was, the best play for the last hand was to be the minimum, not the max. At that stack size, every chip was worth exponentially more. I had confused winning the most with winning more than anyone else. They consoled me that I'd still advance and might even finish top five, I'd done a good job. That seemed funny to me. I was sitting in first by a large margin. After the first half hour, I had something like 110k chips while the next closest had maybe 60k.

I had four hours where I wouldn't need to play, so my only option was to watch the leaderboard. Qualifying on my first hand was both the worst and best thing that could've happened. I gave Ben back his rebuys, since I wouldn't be needing them.

I went up to one of the rooms to relax while everyone else played. I took the opportunity to smoke, but the prospect of three hours up there alone was terrifying. I went back to the casino floor.

I played low stakes poker to keep busy while pacing the same circuit between the poker room and the distant part of the Venetian where the baccarat tournament was held. Each lap took about ten minutes, and I made fifteen laps. I played maybe five hands of poker, spending the entire time cutting around throngs of tourists, observing them idly

Seat Open

chatting, smiling, taking pictures. I couldn't sit, I was full of kinetic, nervous energy.

On my final lap, I checked the leaderboard. I was 4th and disappointed. But I immediately had to bury that disappointment when I heard how everyone else did. Melanie, Greg, and Joe John had barely qualified for the next round. Jimmy qualified, but to do so he had needed ~100 rebuys. Almost $10,000 to win back $500, but also the chance to play for more. Whenever something like that happens, you never know who to feel worse for—the backer or the backed.

I was guaranteed a few thousand for my finish, so I shut my mouth and followed the MC's directions to collect my prize with the rest of the "winners." It was tough to be upset.

Player Two

I had thrown a "21" reference around earlier—an allusion to the Hollywood-glossed story of an MIT math club that conquered Vegas with blackjack strategies— and we all laughed. But after open play, Jimmy mentioned another "crew."

The UNLV Math Club, like a bad joke, had put together a team of eight scrappy mathematicians from their undergrad and graduate ranks. They even had a professor with them, part-advisor/part-chaperone. Furthermore, their de-factor leader Aaron was a poker player. He and Jimmy shared mutual friends. The team was even partially backed from Aaron's poker bankroll.

We couldn't help but see the UNLV team as a bizarro version of ourselves. But poker forces one to reckon with truth, and in truth, we were the bizarro version of them. They were the polo and khaki-clad kids who went to class and studied. Used their talents for good. We skipped school to gamble. Used our talents to get ahead. We each thought we were better, but we were only different.

As Jimmy was filling us in, two Asian men approached and interrupted him. A younger guy in sweatpants, and an older man in a sharp suit. The younger one rushed up, talking a mile a minute, and we realized he was star struck. Jimmy, it turned out, was his favorite poker player.

The older man introduced himself as a casino host. The younger kid was a rich whale on his way to or from the baccarat table and wanted desperately to meet Jimmy. The host did a perfect job of pretending to know who everyone was. We took pictures of the kid and Jimmy, then the host calmly wrote our group a $500 comp to any restaurant in the Venetian. I couldn't imagine how much this kid lost that his passing interest warranted such an expensive gift. It felt silly, all that money passing around so freely, none of it belonging to anyone there.

We changed our plans from another Grand Lux trip to a booth at Delmonico, our preferred steakhouse at the Venetian. No one seemed phased by the encounter. By now we knew that sometimes things just happened like that. Jimmy, resident foodie, ordered for us and we stuffed ourselves with rich cuts of meat before we went back to our rooms with curtain-drawn windows and set alarms to gamble for Macau.

Group Play

The next day we met at the Wheel of Fortune machines. We saw the UNLV Math Team with their hoodies and hats. Their Chaperone-Guide was giving them a pep talk near their own Lord of the Rings slots.

The next segment of the tournament was our "Final Jeopardy" stage.

Everyone who advanced from yesterday needed to win their table of four to advance to the American

Seat Open

championship, later that day. Multiple entrants at the same table was a curse for us, since it meant someone was forced to not qualify. Unfortunately, we had two tables of two. But other than that, we looked well-poised for the next round and more prize money.

We took our seats.

I drew two older Asian women and an Asian man that looked like a lifetime gambler. I wasn't sure if it was the Super Bowl XXVI shirt, or the fact that he had a tiny notebook to, like a baseball diehard, manually track the movements of the game. Upon further inspection, all three of my opponents had a notebook. They looked at me like I was an imbecile for not bringing my own tea leaves to read.

The dealer handed out paper folders, to be used for the last hand, propped up to hide your final, uncapped wager. Just like final jeopardy. My pulse quickened. This was serious. Jimmy and Ben played later so they stood behind me, doing their best to observe, incidentally breathing down my neck. Every hand was its own battle, strategically planned and executed, each with an element of tragic uncertainty. We bet cautiously.

By the fourth hand, the Asian man had gambled with a big bet, lost, and was too afraid to try and catch up. I stuck to the group's strategy, avoided bad luck, and got to the final hand as chipleader. I double-checked my tally of chips.

61k v 49k v 38k v 36k

But now I had to size my final bet. I was in brain lock. Stuck in my head, I thought about the Asian woman in second place, who flipped her eyes up at me from under her old-timey gambler's visor. I checked my math, double-checked my math, thought about all the possible outcomes of all the possible bets. My head was spinning. Everyone else had locked in their wagers. They were waiting on me.

I apologized to the table for taking so long and wrote down my bet. We took down our protective shields. I heard Jimmy from behind me say, "Oh, thank God," and knew I made the right play.

I had bet Banker. But I didn't get the right cards. Player won, 7-5. The Asian woman made the right play and took the other side, winning our table. I stood up frustrated, a loser, and went back to my group.

I was disappointed, but Jimmy and Ben assured me I played the best I could've, and I was just unlucky. Jimmy said he got worried when I was taking so long. I asked how long I had sat there. I thought maybe five or ten minutes.

"About half an hour," he told me.

Championship

The tournament continued without me. Our group didn't fare as well as we hoped. Our six advancers were whittled down to three. That was after an especially brutal hand between Ben's friend Rodney and UNLV captain Aaron, where Aaron spiked a 10% card to eliminate Rodney and advance UNLV in one fell swoop.

Inevitably, our losing players gravitated to the UNLV team's losing players. I was approached by their only female member, Bayley. As she struck up conversation, she was little interested in me, but very interested in my team's betting strategies. Through her I learned her team's story, including how their backer knew some of us already, who they were, how they got started, and why they were there. I think she initially tried to work as a honeypot, but got caught up in the excitement of their success and couldn't stop talking,

The final table was set, probably the size of three poker tables formed into one massive felt-covered behemoth. The mood was akin to the championship round of a middle school chess tournament. Dreams of individual glory were

Seat Open

dashed, but the hopes of the team stayed alive. Our team had three (Jimmy, Greg, and Melanie,) the UNLV group had three (including Aaron and Bayley). All I could do now was watch.

An MC was given a microphone to wrangle the crowd and introduced the players. Play began and started painfully slow. No one wanted to be the first to mess up and everyone bet the minimum. Of the first ten rounds, seven felt like charades. Despite playing baccarat for thousands of dollars hours ago, I could barely follow the action on the giant table. God forbid I actually advanced. I would've looked like three kids in a trench coat.

Finally, fireworks popped. Players bet larger portions of their stacks and fortunes shifted. Jimmy, Greg, and Melanie made their big bets, but as each round played out, they lost; and the UNLV Team stacked more and more chips. By the last hand, Ben clarified for me—we needed a lot of luck... and we didn't get it. The UNLV Team had secured 1st and 3rd through a string of ties and bonus bets. We weren't advancing. The good guys had won.

Victory Lapse

We consoled each other. The important baccarat was over, but we weren't completely finished. We collected our prize money in cash, but had bonus promotional chips, between $500 and $1500 each (not redeemable for cash value, of course), to gamble through and try and turn into real money. Every $100 won was awarded in a real chip. The only rule was never bet the real chip.

We went to a high-stakes baccarat table, still dejected, hoping to make it quick. We didn't have a reason to be in the casino, or even Las Vegas, and quickly felt like average gamblers. Tourists.

We tried to bet both sides of the same hand, to hedge our downside, but the management gestapo caught on fast and we were forced to take our chances straight-up. Betting $200 of promo chips per hand surrounded by straight-from-Macau degenerates, squeezing each card with gross anticipation, was nothing short of withering. Taxing on the soul.

    We broke even on the promos. We were starving and chose the one food we'd all agreed on—sushi. We drove far from the casino. Ben paid and we all ate until we were sick. Despite Ben not winning his millions, I knew there were more bullets in the chamber. I felt most bad for Jimmy. He was the de facto assistant coach of the team and, like all assistant coaches, he wanted the win most.

    I had no idea what happened to the UNLV team after they took their obligatory picture with their big, phony check, although I truly hoped they scooped 1st and 2nd in Macau. If not us, them.

    In the end, Ben mostly broke even. I stuffed enough to cover a few months of rent into my backpack. Everyone got a great story. And two years later, like all legitimate bad guys, we came back for the sequel.

Seat Open

The Ruby Dragon Baccarat Championship (2018)

A woman with blue hair crooned "Smooth Operator" with a timbre that made you stop and shut your eyes. I hadn't been back to Vegas for months and had never been to this nearly-empty wine bar in my life. Apparently, it had some of the best hummus in the city. Another desperate attempt for Las Vegas to stay relevant. Regardless, the live music was on point.

I saw Jimmy at a large booth, laptop out on the table to present to the team. Jimmy was sitting with Ben and wearing his signature newsie cap, which he had the large frame to actually pull off.

Ben had been gracious enough to invite me for the next iteration of the baccarat team. The tournament hadn't been worthwhile to invest in heavily in 2017, but this year offered much better opportunity. I didn't know how many others we were waiting for as I flipped through a menu. It hurt to see that most of the people in the restaurant were at our table. The talented hipster singing by the front door deserved a more attentive audience.

All of our focus was on Jimmy's PowerPoint. Jimmy had taken a more official co-captain position, happily buying some of the team's financial exposure with bitcoin profits. Now, he prepared a slideshow to go over the tournament schedule, training, and strategy review. Our baccarat crew had gone from a ragtag guerilla outfit to a well-oiled betting machine. Jimmy mentioned we'd be tweaking payouts this year because of some "shadiness" that had occurred. I knew better than to ask. Public inquisition into a resolved dispute was verboten in gambling culture.

Blockhead

Jimmy emailed PDF study guides to look at after lunch. The tournament started the next day. We filled each other in on life updates, potential investments, and new Vegas restaurants. Like old times, Ben paid the bill.

We went outside to the cars, and I waited for an Uber in the shade. It was scorching hot outside, 108 degrees, another bleak Vegas summer. The sun burned, so it made you squint to even stand outside. You could be staring at a dirt lot, or cars across the asphalt, and you'd have to wince from the sheer heat of it all.

I had two friends from law school in town for a bachelor party, so not only would I be playing a baccarat tournament, but I'd be making recurring appearances at Hooters, the strip club, or wherever else these wayward Midwesterners journeyed.

My Uber dropped me off where my lawyer friend Jeff was staying, the MGM; the scene of my infamous high school hotel party.

I walked through the visual mishmash of the casino. It used to be Alice in Wonderland themed. The owners vaguely changed the look to Hollywood-esque at some point but seemed to be hyper aware of Planet Hollywood just up the street and stopped décor just short of comprehensive. The results: nighttime in an old Hollywood mansion. Everything gold and shiny.

I waited in the lobby for Jeff and Justin. Jeff had entered law school after a career as a geological engineer, which meant he had an appreciation for the finer things in life, and he came in with clear perspective. Some of my fondest memories with Jeff were in the passenger seat of his M5 listening to stories of dating Brazilian supermodels. Jeff was staying at the SkyLofts, though I doubted he would be incurring any fees.

Jeff and Justin met me in the lobby. Justin had matured since law school, the result of an intense job as a trial

Seat Open

lawyer for a large insurance firm. He had graduated from smooth-talking law student to smooth-talking litigator.

The three of us ate dinner at a steakhouse in the hotel. Brady, the bachelor, came by drunk, in a Hawaiian shirt, but only for a moment. He dropped off another one of their party—Dave. Dave, it turned out, was an emotional Achilles of the group; the one who routinely drank too much. Despite being a software developer for a large California marijuana dispensary (a sweetheart job, if I'd ever heard it), Dave had it bad.

Just before the bachelor party, in a twist of depressing irony, Dave's fiancé broke up with him. He also lost his driver's license after his third DUI in an attempt to cope with the pain. He was like Ed Helms in The Hangover, but with sadder alcoholism and none of the fictitious charm. I tried to keep him at arm's length.

Fittingly, as Dave was telling us his woes, we drank like fish. I had been working on my alcohol intake, but drinking with lawyers was hard. I was eager to get a meal in me. The waitress approached. Without so much as tensing a muscle, Jeff said, "There's enough rye in the Manhattans, we don't need the bread."

I had missed his quips, even if it meant a hangover in the morning. She smiled and turned away, leaving me with just a liquid appetizer.

Drunk, I Ubered back to Jimmy's house where I was staying. I took Ben's room while he stayed in a hotel. Ben still maintained his SevenStar VIP status and slept in hotels most days of the year because, frankly, why wouldn't he?

Walking into the house, I could also see why. They were straddling the line between charming degenerate and messy. Jimmy was busy setting up a new business, training a puppy, and pampering his other Dachshund. The dogs ran his life while he ran the company. There was another roommate that played Magic: The Gathering full-time and compounded on the clutter.

I went to the spare room and unpacked—I saw an ant. Then another. Then an entire moving column of ants, streaming from the bathroom to a window nearby. I remembered Jimmy had told me there was an ant problem in their neighborhood. There were so many, tightly organized. I killed and cleaned ant corpses for two hours. I saw it as a feat of discipline.

Day 1

Jimmy and I carpooled to the Venetian. He drove the same blue sports car he had since I'd met him, to me symbolizing the halcyon days of poker. He took it to get serviced often. The seats were worn thin.

We walked through the casino and a blackjack dealer waved at us. He and Jimmy made small talk. They talked about Jimmy's Instagram-famous dogs, and Jimmy and I continued on our way. I thought Jimmy was just being friendly, but he actually recognized the guy.

It took Jimmy a bit to place him, but he remembered. They both used to live at the Panorama—one of Vegas' notable gambler-filled condos. The dealer was also a Dachshund owner.

"It's hard to remember so many dealers," Jimmy said.

It always amazed me that dealers were amongst the highest earners in the city. Easy in a town that shunned creativity. Las Vegas built its first major performing arts theatre in 2012. Its first Wicked performance came soon thereafter. These were not people that troubled themselves with fictions.

"Hanging out with your friends, trying to beat the casino, is a great fucking feeling." Jimmy bobbed through the crowd. He was excited. I was, too. I was eager for a chance to redeem my 4th place finish from two years ago.

Seat Open

We arrived at the tournament area to see the event already underway. One dozen self-scanners hummed, overseen by friendly staff, waiting to print our entry tickets. It seemed we weren't the only ones who had upgraded from years before. Jimmy handed out rubber-banded stacks of money and zip-locks for receipts. More protection, to make sure everyone was compensated fairly.

A floor man standing by helped me learn the computerized registration process the first time through. By the third or fourth rebuy, I'd be flying through the confirmation screens. The staff enjoyed this. They by-and-large loved us. They remembered Jimmy and Ben from their previous successes.

We fanned out and there were already sixty or seventy people filling twenty-four baccarat tables. Some were there to play multiple times but many, because it was the first and biggest day of the event, were only there for their one free entry. Unfortunately, part of the rules dictated after a receipt check at each table, dealers were forced to explain the rules to the entire tournament before play began.

This wasn't so bad one time, but after your fifth or thirty-fifth entry, hearing the rules to baccarat made you want to die. In practice, the dealers mostly bet for the new players, just asking which side they wanted to move all-in on. I was thankful one of the key points of our strategy was going all-in on the first hand. Half the time, our matches lasted barely a minute.

I was hoping to repeat my run from the last tournament and qualify in the first hand. Anything, so long as I didn't "pull a Jimmy" from last year and spend thousands in entries. Unfortunately, we had forgotten to include being lucky in our strategy guide.

Table 1:
I suffered through the betting instructions, trying my best to ignore them. A middle-aged white man who looked

like he had done this before sat next to me. There was a nervous energy that immediately disappeared as we both won our first hand. He mostly followed my bets, and we made it through all ten hands unscathed. He (201k) cashed for a little more than I did (170k) and shouted to a previously unseen teammate, watching from behind him on the rail. I approached Jimmy nearby, but he was well-armed to evaporate any illusions of success I had. "That won't even be close for top 20." It would be a long day.

Table 2:

I sat across an Asian woman in a red dress with yellow dragons on it and an Asian man in a red, plaid shirt. Most of the décor this year was yellow and red, again. I had flashbacks of the bizarre looking polo from 2016 somewhere at the bottom of my closet. The man in plaid and I lost the first hand betting on Banker. I quickly found an open table and he slipped into a seat next to me. At table 3, the man in plaid and I bet on opposite sides. I lost. It was obvious he didn't realize his shirt was unlucky.

Tables 4 – 6:

I was in the corner of the roped off playing area and the dealers saw my stack of rebuy receipts— that I knew what I was doing— and let me play tables quickly before the MC filled them with players from the long line. Vegas is a city built on nepotism. Returning to line was a thorn in the side of each of us playing for Ben. Because we followed identical betting strategies, playing at the same table limited our returns. We were forbidden from playing together. This meant we were capped by the flow of the line and often led to two or three of us dawdling in the slot machines nearby, not wanting to be grouped up with each other.

Table 10:

Seat Open

I was led to a table full of South American cougars. One of them let a smile linger. As the dealer matched our IDs with our registration receipts, I took a shot. I had already lost so much. "You should check their IDs twice, make sure the ink is dry." As soon as I said the line, I knew it was dead on arrival. I was still in my 20s. Some things, like fedoras, needed the age. Fortunately, I busted the next hand and didn't look back. Jimmy flagged me down. Our friend Rick had arrived, and Jimmy asked if I could bring him up to speed on the rules. I was a little surprised, the least math savvy tasked with teaching an entire game. I showed him everything I knew, which wasn't much, and he filled in the gaps with research on his phone. It was a simple strategy and at this stage, our only enemies were time and fatigue. I wished him luck and we hopped into the fray.

Table 14:
I sat down at what felt like a sitcom. A middle-aged man with a pencil thin mustache and a hawkish woman (yes, in a red dress) conferred with a bulky white man, who looked like a bulldog, dripping in gold chains. He wore a loud Union Jack polo, taken from a Guy Richie movie. It was a moment before I realized—they were another team, trying their best, competing against us for glory. They didn't realize they were minimizing their own effectiveness by playing together, nor that they had no effectiveness with no strategy. Watching them made me depressed.

Table 17:
I sat with three other regulars I met at various points in the night. By now, we had shed most of the newbie players. The dealer, a man named Kenneth, made a joke about teaching us the rules as he hurried to get us started. Kenneth was tall and tan with a thick head of black and grey hair. His hometown was listed as Bronx on his nametag, and I guessed he went by 'Yo, Kenny!' growing

up, at a time when A-tops were still called wifebeaters. I was parched and looked past Kenneth to the dealer station. Normally empty, the podium was stacked with snacks and juices for the dealers to grab on their downtime, like marathon runners getting relief. What was a grind for us was work for them, and they came prepared. Kenneth caught me staring at a pallet of water bottles with thirsty eyes.

"Here," he said, and grabbed me one. I thanked him and cracked open the lid, chugging gulps like a middle schooler at peewee football. All the money flying around and the most notable exchange over the past hour was for an 8-oz bottle of water.

Tables 19 – 24:
One hand busts. Every table. I couldn't help but give a half-smile and shrug, peeling off $50 receipts like tickets to a charity raffle.

Table 25:
I was back at Kenneth's table with three Asian grinders. They each had a scoring sheet, used to track the sequence of cards as they came out. This was common amongst some of the "pro" players and also common in the Asian circles. There was no correlation between the two. One them offered me a sheet, which I should've taken with kindness, but instead smiled and shook my head. My three tablemates laughed at my rebuff. One of them rattled off a joke in Chinese and they laughed again. I didn't mind, feeling like I was being mocked by the homeless for not believing in the Rat King. But in what I can only describe as "American-accented Chinese," Kenneth admonished the group for picking on me. My eyes went wide. I supposed it made sense, a man working with Chinese whales all day needed to communicate with them fluently. Nonetheless, Kenneth's Mandarin was totally unexpected.

Seat Open

The MC told us play was wrapping up for the day. I burned through the rest of my entries and found the group. Everyone crowded around the leaderboard and I saw why—Rick, who I had tutored only hours prior, had 1st prize secured with 540k chips.

I was speechless. I had unknowingly passed my torch of beginner's luck to Rick. First prize was $10,000, plus round two entry, and a trophy. I'd be lying if I said I wasn't jealous. With Rick's win the group had done incredibly well. We had several cashes and two in the top three advancing. I lost some money, but tomorrow brought a new session.

Our Grand Lux tradition held strong. We piled into a massive booth with something like a dozen of us. My head was still buzzing from the past four hours of non-stop baccarat. This wasn't like last year, one hand and done. Every deck, every decision, processing software still trying to catch up despite sitting now in the marble palace of the Cheesecake Factory clone. Joe John, as if two years ago were only yesterday, unfolded a napkin and took out two Luna bars. His entire dinner. I almost couldn't believe it.

That night, I carpooled back with Jimmy. I felt a perfect fatigue I hadn't felt since being a poker player. I wanted a distraction, so I watched the newest episode of Big Brother. Fessi broke his alliance with Kaitlyn and used his veto power to save Hayleigh. I guess you couldn't trust anyone.

Day 2

Nerves woke me early, so I worked out. It was a blessing Ben had a bench and weights in his room. I needed sanity.

Today, the bachelor party was at the Hooters casino. I took an Uber to meet Jeff and Justin. The depression of the ten-table gaming pit was both totally expected and completely surprising. The whole bachelor party was there, and I was finally able to meet everyone in the sober light of day. We moved out from the air-conditioned casino to the mostly outdoor bar next to the pool.

The group were hearty Chicagoans. Someone mentioned, unprompted, that I should bulk up. We ordered pizza and beer and reveled in its shittiness. It was 110 degrees and even though I didn't want to look like a pussy, I had to borrow someone's sandals to walk across the scalding hot cement to the pool. I was too much of a coward for third degree burns.

Even caked in sunscreen, my body was under attack from the temperature. Human beings were not meant to exist in these conditions. Jeff and I sat in the pool and talked. The Hooters pool wasn't anything special, but the heat gave it an apocalyptic feel. People skittered along the concrete like beetles from shadow to shadow, mostly staying by the bar. The fact that there were outdoor air-conditioned bars in the desert said more about Las Vegas than I ever could.

The pressure of a full day of baccarat bore down upon me. I looked at my phone. I already had to leave. My sunbaked brain thought I could walk from Hooters to the Venetian, which was about as tourist of an idea as ordering a prostitute from the hotel concierge. I made it half a block and called an Uber. At the Venetian, I picked up money from Jimmy and bought another dozen entries, hoping that was all I'd need.

At my first table, I met a man wearing a white fedora who was, in fact, old enough to pull it off. He smiled at me and picked up— either from my rubber-banded stack or comfortable posture—that I was a regular. He immediately talked about the casino, how much he liked this tournament, and Punto Banco, which was evidently what we were playing.

Seat Open

"Punto Banco is the more relaxed version of baccarat. They play it down south."

He didn't mean Texas. Having played baccarat in the pit, I knew there were small differences in the game. I thanked him for the bit of trivia. Sometimes these morsels of facts are all you're given for hours at a time in a casino. You adapt and learn to sustain yourself off them.

Fedora tied me with 400k chips. I smiled at him, only a little miffed and moved to the next table. I saw his name again on the leaderboard with 310K. He was definitely a professional of sorts. Good for him.

At the next table, I sat with what appeared to be a Brazilian family. Mother, dignified with shoulder-length hair, a daughter about my age, and a father wearing double-wrist supports. I took a seat next to the daughter.

They said they had never played baccarat before. The father said they were all "virgins" and he gave me a look that, frankly, I had no idea what to do with. I started with the same bet I'd made at every table, all-in on Banker, and I used a line for when I wanted to impose a mood on the table.

While I slid the chips on the Banker tile, I looked at the daughter and said, "Good luck, Player." Something about wishing for my own downfall always prompted smiles.

"You look like you know what you're doing," the father said.

I thought about pushing it, but being on the clock, I passed. Anyway, I lost, congratulated them on being luckier than me, and moved to the next table.

A few hours later, Rick showed up. He carried a tiny gift bag with his trophy inside. He took out a bright red box and opened it. Inside, sitting on a mound of yellow fabric, was a dark, orb-shaped statue. On closer inspection, it was a large dragon decal in the design of a yin-yang, details obscured in dark turquoise and black. I wanted a trophy more than anything.

Blockhead

The woman in the red dress from yesterday with the English Bulldog Man was there. While I was moving between tables, she waved me over. When I came near, she physically grabbed my collar and pulled me aside, staring into the distance. The interaction was almost seductive.

She leaned in to where I felt her breath on my cheek and told me, "Naturals are jumping around."

She was trying to tell me that an element of the game— natural nine, instant wins— was occurring more often than it should. Superstitious nonsense.

"It's not about the table streak, it's your streak."

She spoke like a zealot. Like she knew God. She was dangerous. I was intrigued.

The pencil mustache from her team appeared near us on the rail. He passed me a scorecard. It looked like hieroglyphics. I wanted to tell him that it wasn't this complicated. He needed to think a little more and a little less. Did they know the game wasn't even baccarat, but the more delightful 'Punto Banco'?

I smiled and thanked him after clearly not having taken enough time inspecting his card of fortune. I was met with looks of intimidation. To this team, we represented the baccarat equivalent of the Spanish Inquisition. My faith in divine mathematical process was unsettling. The woman in the red dress claimed, "You only rely on luck!" Maybe, but not all who wander are lost.

Our team ended up with a strong showing, Darren securing 2nd place. Unfortunately, there was other news— Aaron's UNLV team was back. This time, however, it was only a skeleton crew— just Aaron and his father-in-law. I imagined the rest of the players had taken jobs at Google or Apple. Talked about the baccarat tournament as a bit of funny personal trivia. Regardless, Aaron was on the leaderboard. It almost made me sad, like the last bandmate playing songs from an earlier era. I wondered what that said about us.

Seat Open

At the apartment, the ants were back. I couldn't buy Raid because of the dogs, so I fought them off by hand. I built a wall with Gabe's dirty clothes, months old. The ants moved back and forth from a hole in the floor, to the window, seeming content to honor the boundary. There could be dozens or millions; I didn't know, but it didn't seem like they would bother me. They had grander plans. I shut off the lights and laid in bed thinking about an entire bustling colony of ants underground. I slept uneasily.

Day 3

Two more days of tournament remained.
There was a storm on the drive. Like all desert storms, it was powerful. They roamed like giants, doing what they may. They were like storms in the South without the protection of any environment. No Spanish moss where under you could listen to the rain.
Jimmy and I carpooled again. Early in the day, I ran back to the car, having forgotten my phone. When I returned to the tables, I saw Kenneth. He had an open seat, so I sat. Jimmy came by to pick up his car keys and Kenneth made the connection.
"I shoulda realized you were part of his crew," Kenneth said to me.
"I'm too smart not to be."
At this point, I felt closer to Kenneth than any other person on Earth. There was something to be said for how the dealers openly cheered on our team without a hint of irony. They didn't have a stake in the matter—they got paid either way. But we provided a type of entertainment for them. People loved stories and, moreover, they loved underdogs. Rather than lose ourselves to the static of the machinery, we engaged with them. Established a bond. Created a narrative. Or maybe it was the other way around.

I signed more entry receipts. I had the process down to where no one could've done it faster. My signature was a spasm. The dealers watched me fly through my stack. I pretended this wasn't the part I did best.

I sat a few tables but didn't manage anything. Jonny, a fast-talking Filipino dealer waved me over. He enjoyed us and was always willing to help get a quick table in when he could. He was one of our bigger fans.

"C'mon, c'mon," he hurried me.

I tossed him one of the sheets as he started dealing. I felt good, just him and I.

I won the first hand.

"Okay, there we go," he muttered. We were still a long way from home.

Then I won the second hand. I kept betting the max, following the strategy. I won five of the next six hands and on my eighth hand I froze. What the fuck was I supposed to bet?

Last week's practice was years in the past and my brain couldn't think beyond the hours of fizzled baccarat hands I had sat through. I couldn't remember if I was supposed to bet the minimum or the maximum.

I saw Joe John staring at me from an adjacent table. He eyed my stack and smiled, cool and confident. He knew what to do. He thought I was just taking my time. I tried to force telekinesis. Surely those Luna bars were good for something.

I had 425k chips. I hadn't checked the leaderboard in a few minutes, although I knew I was likely in first. But by how many? What if I wasn't? I wouldn't get this opportunity again. I looked at my chips. More than anything, I didn't want a repeat of last time. Punting my stack had been tragic. My instinct then, like now, was bet it all. The siren call of Gamble Gamble.

Seat Open

I slid a meager 1k chip into the betting circle. Matt smiled and nodded. Betting the minimum, I had done good. I won that hand, lost the next, and won the last.

426k chips. I was in first place. Here we go again. I was both in a position of dominance and utterly exposed to anyone on a lucky streak.

I passed Kenneth's table and he called out. "Is that you at the top?" Either he recognized my last name or was genuinely hopeful.

"Yup."

"Well alright then." Kenneth let shine a full, relieved smile. This gave me an immediate insight into his personal life. In his pleasant, subdued response, I saw a man who tried his best and was likely a decent husband or father.

My calmness was short-lived as Jimmy waved me over to another table. He hovered behind Aaron's father-in-law. The UNLV team, again, trying to upset us. I could tell he had a lot of chips— maybe more than me, I wasn't sure— and he was on his final hand. He was calculating a bet.

Oh no.

This meant he was so close he didn't want to risk single chip more than he needed. He carefully counted out and slid forward a stack of chips. I was a 50/50 to win. The hand was dealt, his bet on banker.

And he won.

There was a massive high-five from Aaron, and I immediately tried to make myself content with 2nd place. $6,000 instead of $10,000. But there was a murmur at the table. Aaron shook his head. Jimmy leaned over to me and whispered, without making eye contact, "425."

"But he didn't bet the max, he counted his bet out." I argued, certain of my defeat.

"Misclick."

He had made a mistake. My anxiety vanished. All that practice and time, and evidently, Aaron's father-in-law bet a single 1K chip less than he meant. Maybe he confused my

Blockhead

stack, maybe he miscounted. It didn't matter. The crisis was averted. My throne was safe.

We hung around as play wrapped up for the day. No tables had any games left. I was the day's top scorer. I made Ben money. I had won my own trophy.

On our way out, the dealers gave a round of applause, cheering us on. I had the familiar feeling of success I learned from poker, the opposite of failure, numb relief.

We thought about eating at the Grand Lux a third night, but frankly no one had it in them.

From his earlier win, Darren had $500 of promo money to play through. This year we weren't playing at the baccarat tables, but the high-limit slots. Sitting with Jimmy, watching the rapid-fire animations of spades and hearts, I texted a few friends that I won. They congratulated me. I wandered the small, private high-limit area. Glistening $5 minimum slots that were empty and likely always that way. In a nearby machine, I saw: CREDIT: $12.50

Forgotten or simply deemed not worth the hassle. I cashed out the free money. When it rains, it pours.

The bachelor party had a full night planned. Ready to take the edge off, I met up with them between dinner and a session of drunk gambling. I slid in next to Justin and Jeff at the craps table. Dave and the rest of the party came down and joined us. The group as a whole lost money, something about the collective expectations of a bachelor party weighing too heavily on the table and scaring the good luck away. In these sorts of situations, the best thing that can happen is someone usually unnoticed—the groom's brother— sneaks into massive luck. I didn't tell them about my baccarat win.

Sufficiently drunk and battered, we went to the nightclub. A host had been contacted and a VIP table arranged. While this may seem like it meant exclusivity, it really just meant we stood in front of a line separate from general admission—one of six or seven lines— packed

Seat Open

with some men in various shades of dark, slightly wrinkled button-downs and women in tight dresses. The higher the heel, the more shown skin, the more vacant stares or halfhearted pickup lines pitifully given as praise. Men dashed themselves on icy demeanors like monks to a big, stone Buddha.

We were led by a bouncer, past a series of checkpoints, through a labyrinth of velvet ropes and dark halls to our table. The club was packed and by the time we sat down, I was completely disinterested. I knew the bachelor party would get into some trouble, but I didn't want a part of it. I was exhausted from three days of baccarat, and some drunk gambling was enough for me. I let the group know and they didn't mind. I left the club only needing to ask for directions once.

Day 4

Another desert storm. Rain came down in sheets. Having both already qualified, Jimmy and I were only stopping at the Venetian to pick up my trophy.

Justin texted me updates about Dave. Apparently, the night had turned sour shortly after I left. Dave got trashed, which wasn't a surprise, and somehow convinced Justin and Jeff to leave for Drais, an after-hours club, where Dave met with escorts and spent the next hour in unproductive negotiation. I was glad I missed it.

Jimmy and I parked and greeted everyone still playing. I watched them bounce between tables, betting the same strategy over and over. It could've been me. I was thankful it wasn't. I picked up my trophy at the registration desk. I opened it to inspect. It was both identical to Rick's and marvelous all on its own.

I went back over to the tournament area to spectate. Three people that I recognized approached. The Brazilian

Blockhead

family from the day prior. The daughter, smiling. "How did you do yesterday?"

I held up my trophy.

"Congratulations!" She let out a cry and hugged me, planting a kiss on my cheek. I considered asking what her plans were later, impressing parents, getting a phone number. But some interactions are too fragile to observe. She smiled and they continued off.

I found Jimmy and we went back to the car. We headed back to his house. I had to go back to LA soon. I was exhausted, but felt fulfilled, looking down at the trophy—my success—between my feet.

I wouldn't know it then, but we wouldn't actually play the next round. The tournament staff changed their entire structure making it disadvantageous for us to continue. We had won too much money. Ben told us it wasn't worth our time, and if there's one thing I had learned in a decade of gambling, it was to bet on Ben.

Jimmy saw me typing trip notes into my phone.

"This'll make a good story, huh?" he asked.

"All those degenerates with their scorecards. It's crazy," I told him. But Jimmy only shrugged.

"You think about people a lot more than I do."

I smiled at him. Jimmy made himself a millionaire at 19. It took a lot to impress him. Still, I had one thing.

"The craziest part," I said, "without a doubt, was finding out Kenneth spoke fluent Chinese."

Jimmy turned to me.

"Who's Kenneth?"

Acknowledgements

This book would not exist without:
Gabe, backing me in one form or another for years, and Mike & Jenn—the family, Jessi's wellspring of support, Jimmy's tutelage, Team Nihar, Ann's editing and patience, Chunk's cover design, the beta readers and supportive cretins of the Architects, Justin's legal advice, my therapist, and Kenneth.
Free Brandon.

Author Bio

Blockhead was a former professional poker player, baccarat tournament freelancer, and unlicensed attorney. He is currently a screenwriter in Los Angeles.

You can follow him on Twitter:
@OhYouBlockhead

or e-mail him at:
ohyoublockhead@protonmail.com

Made in the USA
Columbia, SC
28 June 2020